The Balance of

in South Asia

The Balance of

POWER

in South Asia

THE EMIRATES CENTER FOR STRATEGIC STUDIES AND RESEARCH

THE BALANCE OF POWER IN SOUTH ASIA

Published by
The Emirates Center for Strategic Studies and Research
PO Box 4567
Abu Dhabi
United Arab Emirates

e-mail: root@ecssr.ac.ae
http: //www.ecssr.ac.ae

Distributed by
Ithaca Press, an imprint of Garnet Publishing Ltd
8 Southern Court
South Street
Reading
RG1 4QS

ISBN 0 86372 267 9

First Edition

British Library Cataloguing-in-Publication Data
A catalogue record for this book is available from the British Library

Printed in Lebanon

The opinions expressed in this volume are those of the individual
contributors and do not necessarily reflect the views of the
Emirates Center for Strategic Studies and Research.

The Emirates Center for Strategic Studies and Research

The Emirates Center for Strategic Studies and Research (ECSSR) is an independent research institution dedicated to the promotion of professional studies and educational excellence in the United Arab Emirates (UAE), the Gulf and the Arab world. Since its establishment in Abu Dhabi in 1994, ECSSR has served as a focal point for scholarship on political, economic and social matters. Indeed, ECSSR is at the forefront of analysis and commentary on Arab affairs.

The Center provides a forum for the scholarly exchange of ideas by hosting conferences and symposia, organizing workshops, sponsoring a lecture series and publishing original and translated books and research papers. ECSSR also has an active fellowship and grant program for the writing of scholarly books and for the translation, into Arabic, of works relevant to the Center's mission. Moreover, ECSSR has a large library including rare and specialized holdings, and a state-of-the-art technology center, which has developed an award-winning website that is a unique and comprehensive source of information on the Gulf.

Through these and other activities, ECSSR aspires to engage in mutually beneficial professional endeavors with comparable institutions worldwide, and to contribute to the general educational and scientific development of the UAE.

Contents

Abbreviations and Acronyms

ARF	Asian Regional Forum
ARM	Anti-radar missile
ASEAN	Association of Southeast Asian Nations
AWAC	Airborne Warning and Control
BJP	Bharatiya Janata Party
CTBT	Comprehensive Test Ban Treaty
DRDE	Defence Research and Development Establishment
DRDO	Defence Research and Development Organisation
ECO	Economic Co-operation Organization
ECSSR	Emirates Center for Strategic Studies and Research
FMCT	Fissile Material Cut-off Treaty
GCC	Gulf Co-operation Council
GDP	Gross Domestic Product
GNP	Gross National Product
IAEA	International Atomic Energy Agency
IAF	Indian Air Force
ICBM	Intercontinental Ballistic Missile
IRGC	Iranian Revolutionary Guard Corps
ISI	Inter-Services Intelligence
LCA	Light Combat Aircraft
LoC	Line of Control
MAD	Mutually Assured Destruction
NATO	North Atlantic Treaty Organization
NPT	Non-Proliferation Treaty
OIC	Organization of Islamic Conference
PAF	Pakistan Air Force
PML	Pakistan Muslim League
R&D	Research and Development
RCD	Regional Co-operation for Development
SAARC	South Asian Association for Regional Co-operation

SIPRI	Stockholm International Peace Research Institute
START	Strategic Arms Reduction Treaty
TIFR	Tata Institute of Fundamental Research
UAE	United Arab Emirates
UN	United Nations (Organization)
US	United States (of America)
USSR	Union of Soviet Socialist Republics
WMD	Weapons of Mass Destruction

Introduction

Michael Krepon

The Balance of Power in South Asia

The nuclear tests by India and Pakistan, in May 1998, continue to reverberate in South Asia and beyond, including the Arab Gulf. On a superficial level, the tests merely reaffirmed South Asian nuclear capabilities that appear to have been in place for a decade. On a deeper level, however, much has changed, as is evident by the repercussions on the Gulf region and elsewhere.

The acquisition and demonstration of nuclear capabilities have always prompted a chain reaction. The US nuclear program during World War II triggered the British and Soviet nuclear programs; the Soviet nuclear program gave birth to the French and Chinese nuclear programs; the Chinese nuclear program in turn provided momentum for the Indian and Pakistani nuclear tests; and Israel's nuclear capability is linked in many minds to other weapons of mass destruction (WMD) programs, in the Middle East region.

What are the repercussions of the Indian and Pakistani nuclear tests? Will these effects be limited to the triangular relationship involving China, India and Pakistan? Or will they have a larger adverse impact on non-proliferation regimes, thereby undermining the national security of the Gulf states and other troubled regions? The reasons for the Indian Government's decision to test nuclear weapons after a hiatus of twenty-five years warrant close scrutiny to help forecast further proliferation problems.

The initial reason given for India's test – a threat from China – did not gain wide acceptance either within or outside the country. India and its neighbors are wary of China's military capabilities and political objectives in the long run, but during the past decade, Sino-Indian relations had been moving toward normalization. While the pace of normalization has been slow since Rajiv Gandhi visited Beijing in 1988, modest but useful confidence-building measures have been implemented, such as military notifications and the opening of trading posts along the disputed border. Before the ascent of the Bharatiya Janata Party (BJP) to power in India, neither side had appeared interested in disturbing bilateral ties, and both had been moving very cautiously toward final resolution of the border dispute.

China's extensive support to Pakistan's missile and nuclear programs was also cause for considerable concern in India. Most South Asia specialists however, do not view this assistance as the immediate cause of India's nuclear tests. Beijing's assistance appears to have waned over the past few years, as China has adhered more closely to global non-proliferation norms. (Pakistan's flight test of the Ghauri medium-range missile, for example, derived from the purchase of missiles from North Korea, not China.) Moreover, even with China's prior assistance, many Indian political leaders and scientists continued to doubt Pakistani nuclear capabilities until Islamabad proved them wrong.

Subsequent to the initial public justification, Indian officials offered a somewhat different explanation, focusing on troubling long-term trends within southern Asia. According to Indian government officials, the decision was made sooner rather than later, due to the exigencies relating to the Comprehensive Test Ban Treaty (CTBT) and India's nuclear establishment. This argument placed considerable importance on a special conference of states that have ratified the CTBT, convened in late 1999, where India would further be isolated and pressured.

This perceived diplomatic pincer movement lent weight to the arguments posed by Indian nuclear scientists, who believed that data derived from New Delhi's 1974 test were utterly insufficient to provide a nuclear deterrent. Moreover, the scientific team that generated this data was dying out. Without new data and a new team of nuclear scientists to certify new weapon designs – so the argument went – India could not count on having a viable nuclear deterrent against its neighbors.

There is some logic behind this rationale. No one can predict with certainty the future course of Sino–Indian relations. Moreover, the data derived from the 1974 test might not have been useful for weaponization purposes. Still, these explanations for India's test, like those before it, are not entirely convincing. Moreover, the leveraging capacity of a special conference on the CTBT remains very much in doubt, as three of the five permanent members of the United Nations (UN) Security Council (and more than half of the forty-four countries required for the treaty's entry into force) have yet to ratify it, after which they would gain voting rights and put collective pressure on India. Whatever sense of isolation India might have perceived at a prospective conference of CTBT parties pales in comparison to the loneliness of breaking a global moratorium on nuclear testing.

Within the subcontinent, much credence is paid to Western and especially US plans to cap, roll back and eliminate the nuclear option. Non-proliferation policies that many in Washington view as ineffectual or deeply flawed, are often viewed by New Delhi as sinister. So it was with the CTBT's unprecedented entry-into-force clause, a provision championed most intensely by Russia and China in order to keep their testing options open. In retrospect, this ploy, initially proposed by the government of the United Kingdom, led by John Major, and ineffectually challenged by the Clinton administration, backfired on its supporters.

The Clinton administration's unexpected reversal of 12 years of US opposition to the CTBT was explained as an anti-India ploy. The entry-into-force clause was perceived not just as a pressure tactic directed at India, but as part of a larger plan of political isolation and denuclearization. One year before the conclusion of the CTBT, the Non-Proliferation Treaty (NPT) was extended indefinitely, although not unconditionally. In India, this surprising outcome was widely viewed as unconditional surrender by non-nuclear weapon states. From New Delhi's strategic perspective a noose was tightening around India's nuclear option, and would tighten further unless a quarter-century of hesitancy could be abandoned.

The influence of the Indian nuclear establishment was clearly an important factor in the decision to test. Counter-arguments against testing within that powerful constituency were not leaked to the Indian media and might not have been made strenuously during internal deliberations. After all, the development of a critical chorus within nuclear weapon establishments usually takes time, and is often based on the wisdom that is gained from past experience.

A credible technical case could have been made against the need to test. Crude but workable first generation nuclear bombs could have been devised by India's capable scientists, devices in which India's political leaders could have had high confidence without resorting to detonations. (US scientists managed to do so over 50 years ago, using slide rules rather than computers.) In contrast, the test series carried out by India was quite ambitious, testifying to the latitude given to India's nuclear scientists by a succession of political leaders. Given ambitious requirements for nuclear deterrence, testing was a logical outcome. But this still leaves open the question of why India decided to test in May 1998. For the answer, we must look to explanations other than those given by Indian officials.

Domestic politics in India has become a fractious and painful reality, as is true in many countries. The demise of the Congress Party and the inability of any competing party to establish a national base has led to a succession of coalition governments. India has had seven prime ministers since Rajiv Gandhi made his path-breaking trip to Beijing a decade ago. No coalition has been secure from shifting alliances, with the result that political maneuvering has become a full-time preoccupation, crowding out or politicizing even the most substantive national security matters.

In recent decades, increased nuclear danger has been associated with authoritarian states. In India's vibrant democracy, however, domestic political factors have played a key role in nuclear decision-making. Whether despite, or because of the fractiousness of Indian politics, decisions of national importance usually require the consent of all major parties. This was decidedly not the case with the BJP's decision to conduct nuclear tests in May 1998. Neither opposition parties nor most coalition partners were consulted. Many Indian political figures concluded that domestic politics played a part in the BJP's test calculations. When congratulations for the successful tests were offered by Indian political leaders who were excluded from the decision, it should be noted that they were directed to India's bomb makers, and not to the BJP.

Coalition politics in India has not been edifying. The constant jockeying for power and the fragile nature of control by the Central Government, has projected an image of weakness abroad and led to a sense of considerable unease among Indian elites. In many quarters there were rising concerns that India was becoming weak, and a malleable India might be subject to political coercion by those with stronger wills, economies and military power. Moreover, India's small but vocal contingent of strategic analysts voiced their fear of being pushed around by states with nuclear arsenals – especially China and the United States.

An overt nuclear posture would not only serve to counter percep-tions of weakness, but also confer an enhanced status upon India. This argument is now being tested. Immediately after the tests, BJP leaders and others trumpeted India's new status as a nuclear-weapon state, while calling on members of the club to formally acknowledge this fact. Some demanded renegotiation of the CTBT to accommodate India's concerns. Subsequently, these objectives have been scaled back, popular support for the tests has fallen to slightly more than fifty percent, domestic political fissures have reopened and status seekers have become preoccupied by new security concerns raised by the tests. India's quest for a highly coveted permanent seat on the UN Security Council appears to have been badly damaged, at least for the foreseeable future.

Indian strategic analysts and nuclear scientists wanted to join the selective club of declared nuclear weapon states long before the BJP came to power. Membership, it was claimed, would not only confer status, but also increase bargaining power, provide insurance against powerful potential adversaries and confirm technical calculations.

The advent of the BJP government brought these impulses to fruition. As far as both the core of the BJP and its leadership were concerned, a decision to test was a matter of India assuming its rightful place in the world. The decision was also perceived as a matter of safe-guarding India's security. There is much evidence to suggest that the political as well as national security ramifications of this decision were not considered carefully beforehand. The BJP, unlike prior governments that considered testing but then shied away from the decision, was prepared to take risks, accept the consequences and seize the gains.

The Pakistani rejoinder was widely predicted, but nonetheless instructive. Prime Minister Nawaz Sharif enjoyed far more political support than his Indian counterpart, whose party had received just a quarter of the popular vote. In contrast, Sharif's Pakistan Muslim League (PML) held two-thirds of the seats in the parliament; the power of opposition leader Benazir Bhutto had been greatly diminished by her previous term in office; the office of presidency of Pakistan, once a significant counterweight to the power of the prime minister, had been subordinated by installing a family friend in place of a rival; and the military leadership that had ruled the country for roughly half of its life wanted to remain in barracks unless sorely provoked. Indeed, after the nuclear tests, the Army Chief-of-Staff resigned rather than confront the Prime Minister – an unprecedented step.

From this position of unprecedented political strength, Sharif could conceivably have enjoyed some latitude in responding to the BJP's challenge. Moreover, many assumed that Pakistan did not have to carry out nuclear tests to prove the efficacy of a nuclear warhead design reportedly provided by China. By exercising restraint, Sharif could have isolated India diplomatically, reopened Pakistan's military supply relationship with the United States, and secured new financial support for his faltering economy.

These calculations took a back seat to the imperatives of responding in kind to the gauntlet thrown down by the BJP, securing Sharif's domestic base and reassuring a jittery Pakistani public that the "bomb" was, indeed, in Pakistan's possession and not some fiction perpetrated by untrustworthy governments. Having learned repeatedly not to trust leadership declarations at face value, and having been goaded by the BJP's second most powerful figure to "behave" over Kashmir now that India was a nuclear power, Pakistanis needed to celebrate their own detonations. Two weeks after the Indian tests, they had occasion to do so.

The aftershocks of nuclear testing on the subcontinent are likely to be felt for many years to come, and the Arab Gulf will likely feel the tremors. Damage assessments will depend in part, on subsequent steps taken – within the subcontinent and by key parties to the NPT – to repair breaches and seize new opportunities to reduce nuclear dangers. Definitive conclusions can only come with the passage of time, but some preliminary observations might be offered.

The decisions by the governments of India and Pakistan to carry out nuclear tests did not conform to academic theories of international relations or proliferation in which rational calculations are made almost exclusively on the basis of external threats. While external factors were quite important in the Indian and Pakistani decisions to test, the dominant impulse in both cases appears to have been domestic in origin. The classic security concern of how to deal with a more powerful neighbor was clearly evident in the BJP's decision, but considerations of domestic politics and status were even more evident, as well as a strong desire in Indian elite circles to correct a host of perceived national deficiencies.

Many have come to equate proliferation with authoritarian leadership driven by regional ambitions or by a desire to neutralize the power projection capabilities of those who could thwart such ambitions. This model continues to have validity in the Gulf. In the calculations of a Saddam Hussein, for example, domestic political considerations barely register when the subject is WMD. A nuclear option for Saddam – or his ambitions to retain chemical or biological weapons – appear to be driven exclusively by external considerations: For Saddam, such weapons are useful either to coerce neighbors or to deter hostile coalition building. WMD also give Saddam the ability to deter US military options involving ground forces against his regime.

Clearly, the Indian and Pakistani cases were quite different. While the proliferation dynamics of the subcontinent may not be replicated elsewhere, they nonetheless raise troubling questions. If decisions to acquire nuclear weapons are to be driven mainly by domestic political factors, future instances of proliferation may evolve from political power struggles at home. When this factor coexists alongside serious external threats, there could be powerful incentives for proliferation. In this context, Iran bears close scrutiny.

Every test of a nuclear weapon is a declaration of its possible use. Every state that acquires nuclear weapon capabilities increases tensions with its neighbors with whom it has ongoing disputes. The academic theory that countervailing nuclear weapon capabilities between adversaries promotes stability and security has, regrettably, yet to be proven. Offsetting nuclear weapons *might* have helped to avoid direct US–Soviet conflict during the Cold War, but other important factors also worked against direct conflict. On the other hand, offsetting nuclear capabilities during the Cold War prevented neither proxy wars, nor crises of great intensity involving the superpowers.

This model of deterrence stability may eventually come to pass in South Asia, but it is not true now. The decade of the 1990s, when India and Pakistan possessed covert nuclear capabilities, coincided with increased militancy and tension over Kashmir. In the immediate wake of nuclear detonations, the level of violence in South Asia increased far more. The first summer after India and Pakistan tested nuclear weapons, the level of direct fire across the Line of Control (LoC) dividing Kashmir became far more pronounced. In 1999, Pakistan upped the ante considerably, planning and executing a bold tactical maneuver to seize the heights along the Kargil sector of the Line of Control with the assistance of Mujahadeen groups.

Increased nuclear dangers might serve to prompt India and Pakistan to address the Kashmir dispute more seriously in bilateral negotiations. This would require governments secure enough in their domestic standing and wise enough to plan for a safer future. Until these conditions are met, tensions will continue to remain high over Kashmir. Offsetting nuclear capabilities appear to have freed up unconventional military options, as Pakistan has sought to use the tests and the subsequent increase in violence across the LoC to draw international attention to the Kashmir dispute.

How bad will the fallout from nuclear testing in South Asia be? For the Arab Gulf, much depends on the health of the non-proliferation regimes that were shaken by the nuclear testing in India and Pakistan. Two major powers within the Gulf region – Iran and Iraq – have demonstrated a keen interest in nuclear capabilities, while Israel is universally presumed to have a sophisticated arsenal. Other WMD programs also exist in the region. All of these countries have ballistic missiles. If the nuclear testing by India and Pakistan leads to a marked deterioration in non-proliferation regimes, no region in the globe is likely to be more adversely affected than the Gulf, with the possible exception of Northeast Asia.

Unfortunately, the nuclear tests by India and Pakistan have coincided with other trends that damage non-proliferation regimes. The Comprehensive Test Ban Treaty has been summarily rejected by the US Senate. The formal treaty regimes governing strategic offensive and defensive forces have been weakened. Few now expect the Russian Duma to ratify the Strategic Arms Reduction Treaty (START) II without disabling conditions which are likely to create difficulties in the United States Senate; and the Clinton administration appears to be readying amendments to the Anti-Ballistic Missile Treaty. The process of negotiating and ratifying treaties has become unusually extended, and now lags far behind the growth of nuclear dangers in Russia. The seepage or sale of fissile materials (or even intact nuclear warheads) from Russia could have far-reaching negative consequences for the Gulf region and elsewhere.

If the US-Russian strategic arms reduction regime unravels, this will, in turn, weaken the nuclear NPT, which links continued restraint by the 'have nots' with successful efforts by the 'haves' toward the progressive reduction and elimination of their nuclear arsenals. Meanwhile, the CTBT now appears unlikely to enter into force, with Russia, China and Israel yet to ratify the treaty, and with India, Pakistan and North Korea yet to sign it.

The negative trend lines now apparent, feed on one another, which must be welcome news to national leaders who chafe at the constraints imposed by non-proliferation regimes. Indeed, there is already some evidence of opportunistic proliferation following India's decision to conduct nuclear tests: Iran has flight-tested its first medium-range ballistic missile (courtesy, again, of North Korea) and it will be very difficult to reinstitute effective inspection on Saddam Hussein's Iraq. If current trends are not reversed, the national security of states in the Gulf region will be seriously weakened.

This volume, the first of its kind, discusses the impact of nuclear blasts on the subcontinent, in relation to the Arab Gulf. Marvin G. Weinbaum of the US-based Middle East Institute argues that India and Pakistan are trapped in "largely unreconstructed views of strategic defense and national interest," and are consequently suffering the effects of ill-conceived decisions. Weinbaum is skeptical that India and Pakistan can maintain minimum as well as credible nuclear deterrence. Meanwhile, the domestic determinants of national security, which Weinbaum believes are paramount, are likely to wane in influence in New Delhi.

Jasjit Singh of the Institute for Defence Studies and Analyses calls on readers to look beyond South Asia to find a complex, "polycentric" order in which, unfortunately, nuclear weapons and nuclear coercion continue to play a substantial role. Singh dwells on China's future course, which "is heavily loaded with strategic uncertainties." From India's vantage point, the Clinton administration's rapprochement with Beijing is both significant and troubling. Turning to southern Asia, Singh concludes that neither conventional nor nuclear war are viable options for rational leaders. Offsetting nuclear capabilities can, however, lead to continuing sub-conventional war and transnational militancy.

Najam Rafique of the Institute of Strategic Studies in Pakistan traces contemporary difficulties in South Asia to the colonial period, while contending that security problems in South Asia are mostly indigenous. He catalogs the connections between security concerns that are narrowly defined and the problems of health, hunger, poverty, drugs, terrorism and other factors that plague the subcontinent.

Christian Koch of the Emirates Center for Strategic Studies and Research views the nuclear detonations in South Asia as part of the unraveling of the international understandings of the Cold War system. Koch notes that China will cast a large shadow over the newly emerging system. He does not list India among the five primary security concerns perceived by Beijing. Yet China's "strategy of hemming in Indian power and influence" is likely to be complicated by New Delhi's overt nuclear option. Nonetheless, Koch does not anticipate a shift in Beijing's strategy toward New Delhi. It may be difficult to avoid the establishment of a three-cornered nuclear and missile dynamic involving China, India and Pakistan.

Eric Arnett of the Stockholm International Peace Research Institute (Sweden) views South Asia through the dynamic of an ascendant power (India) and a struggling power in descent (Pakistan). Arnett argues that Pakistan's nuclear capability has not altered "the fundamental reality of [its] inferiority and continuing relative decline". India's conventional superiority, in his view, continues to be the dominant strategic factor in the subcontinent. Arnett contends that the risk of war has not been negated by offsetting nuclear capabilities. He believes that it is very much in Pakistan's interest to find a *modus vivendi* on the Kashmir issue.

The final chapter provides a Gulf perspective on the recent nuclear tests in India and Pakistan. In addition to the issue of geographic proximity and the high number of South Asians working in the Gulf, the major concern is possible nuclear proliferation in other countries in the region, such as Iran. The idea of an "Islamic bomb" is rejected and a call for a WMD-free zone in the Middle East is made.

As might be expected in presentations delivered so soon after the Indian and Pakistani nuclear tests, these essays raise many questions and provide few definitive answers. In the immediate aftermath of the tests there is far more uncertainty than clarity. One can be certain, however, that non-proliferation regimes have been weakened, a conclusion that suggests greater danger to the Gulf states.

A special word of thanks is extended to ECSSR editors Herro Mustafa and Mary Abraham for their coordination efforts and editorial input with regard to this volume.

1

The Limits of *Realpolitik* in the Security Environment of South Asia

Marvin G. Weinbaum

Strategic thinking in India and Pakistan is characterized by classic concepts of power and national security, even while these have undergone serious reassessment elsewhere. Both countries continue to employ largely unreconstructed views of strategic defense and national interest. In a relationship shaped mainly by military insecurities and perceived power differentials, the two have adopted policies that distort authentic political-military concerns and devalue their critical social and economic needs. Despite their rich cultural and intellectual traditions, thoughts about the balance of power in India and Pakistan are also strangely lacking in the moral dimension that infuses other areas of their domestic national discourse.

The international scene in South Asia, often characterized as fitting the description of anarchy is used to justify deterrence strategies that are usually associated with *realpolitik* – the drive to accumulate power at the expense of one's adversary. Such thinking focuses most of all on the control of territory and the establishment of spheres of influence or strategic space. Although India and Pakistan decry colonialism and imperialism, they have been willing to rule peoples against their will and exploit others to further national aims. The "Great Game", played first with Russia and then the Soviet Union, may be a thing of the past, but several smaller games are still being played out in South Asia. All of the lingering disputes in South Asia are over territory, most notably the zero-sum game between India and Pakistan over Kashmir.

India is acknowledged to be the dominant power in South Asia, while Pakistan is the challenger, striving to resist India's role as "hegemon".[1] India seeks to be the regional security manager, opposing external power involvement in South Asia. Pakistan, for its part, works to reduce the imbalance through alliances and aid efforts that are intended to inter-nationalize the issues that divide the two countries. In turn, their enmity shapes their relationships with other nations, especially in western and Central Asia, and the Gulf region.

This classic realist's conception of South Asia's state system, in which strategies are designed to gain or hold power, discounts how conflict-mitigating approaches and non-political goals can enhance security. Even a modified formulation of realism for South Asia, which acknowledges the potential of cooperative gains through expanded contacts, tends to be undervalued. Nor is there a full appreciation of the cross-border nature of interests. Having adopted a realist's view of international politics, leaders in the two countries seem determined to make many of the same unfortunate choices as the major international players during the Cold War. The diversion of scarce national resources toward arms escalation and the resort to nuclear deterrence are the most obvious examples. Yet national security for India and Pakistan requires more than the realist's political and military calculations; it must also be assessed in social and economic terms, and threats to the nation must be understood as usually more domestic than foreign in origin. Not uncommonly, policies justified as necessary to the security of the state have instead served to assure the survival of the regime in India and Pakistan and resulted in greater insecurities within the two societies.

Three developments in 1998–99 changed the parameters of conflict and cooperation for India and Pakistan: the emergence of India and Pakistan as declared nuclear weapons states, the Afghan military stalemate, and the Kargil crisis. Although these developments have not altered under-lying regional power equations, they have drawn renewed international attention to the region. For India and Pakistan's neighbors – as well as the rest of the international community, the environment has become more hostile, the region's politics more uncertain and the stakes greater.

Perceptions and the Power Balance

For most of the past half century, military and economic power in South Asia has remained tilted clearly in favor of India. Despite Pakistan's aspirations and efforts, parity has remained beyond its reach. As viewed from Pakistan and the other smaller states in the region, India stands determined to pursue its national goals, often overriding the interests of its neighbors and sometimes interfering with their domestic affairs. These states strive to maintain their capacity to act independently in the shadow of India, and to protect their national interests when these run counter to those of India.

India and Pakistan remain trapped in an antagonism that has changed very little since 1947. Pakistan has never succeeded in separating its foreign policy from its strategic concerns about India. What makes the relationship between India and Pakistan unique among inter-state rivalries is that the terms of their disputes and the accompanying images remain largely fixed. Perceptions that are steeped in history and the emotional trauma of partition often matter far more than any objective reality that involves valid estimates of real and present danger. Perceptions often become self-fulfilling. After 50 years of independence both India and Pakistan are struggling with their insecurities over national identity. As one observer has put it, Kashmir represents a struggle for identity in which "the insecurities of one [country] are exacerbated by the claims of the other."[2] Self-identification is also changing, and legacies are becoming distorted. India's belief in a secular state, offering unity within diversity, is challenged by the BJP's Hindu nationalism. Pakistan has increasingly become a more rigid, less pluralist Islamic state.

Opinions at the elite and popular levels in Pakistan widely hold that India is intent upon undermining and humiliating Pakistan, and would, if it could, reabsorb all of the subcontinent's Muslims. Indians feel that Pakistan is fanatical in its determination to repay India for past defeats, including the loss of Bangladesh, and would like to seize Kashmir in a proxy war. Authorities in New Delhi also view Pakistan as responsible for trying to set the Islamic world (most recently Afghanistan and Central Asia) against India, in order to create a hostile political, military and economic bloc. In turn, Pakistan points to what it sees as evidence of India's hegemonic ambitions and expansionism at the expense of all her smaller neighbors.

Governments in India regularly claim that peace and stability in South Asia require that their country be recognized for its accomplishments and potential. India's leaders contend that their country – as the world's second most populous country, a growing economic and military power, a technological leader and a successful secular democracy – is not given its due status in international forums. The quest for nuclear status is meant to place India on an equal footing with China, as well as oblige those inside the privileged club of nuclear powers to give India the respect it thinks it deserves. Clear feelings of inferiority and resentment exist toward China, and India's embarrassment over the 1962 war with China has never entirely abated.

The failure of India and Pakistan to create confidence-building measures and a normalization of relations reflects this high degree of mistrust between the states and assures continuing suspicions. An improved climate for negotiations in which to resolve differences, or at least introduce conflict-reducing mechanisms, is generally accepted as desirable on both sides. But many in India are wary of any agreements that may have the effect of reducing those advantages that come with a stronger military and political position. Similarly, in Pakistan there is fear that normalization will enable India's better-developed economy to compete unfairly and destroy Pakistan's industry.

India and Pakistan are thus locked into an increasingly expensive political and military competition that ignores the opportunity costs of using the same resources for other purposes. The economies of both countries have been distorted and their development starved by bloated defense budgets. Full investment in nuclear weapons and an assured second-strike capability would, it is estimated, increase total annual defense expenditures in India by at least ten percent.[3] At present, neither India nor Pakistan has the physical or human infrastructure to support a modern economy for most of its citizens, although India has achieved more progress. However, Pakistan and India have been slow to realize their economic potential for other reasons: it has taken an enormous effort for India to extricate itself from a largely centralized economy, while Pakistan, having started at a material disadvantage, has policies that remain hostage to the interests of feudally connected leadership and notoriously corrupt bureaucracy.

The economic compulsions behind liberalizing the economies of India and Pakistan dictate strengthening links to the global economy and greater integration of markets through freer exchange. The cooperation that could bring benefits for economies throughout South Asia is also thwarted by the region's two largest economies. Many had hoped that a regional economic organization would pave the way for greater understanding in the political sphere. However, it is political differences that have driven the relationship while economic cooperation and expected growth have suffered badly.

Domestic pressures contribute toward policies that determine larger strategic choices. Undoubtedly, the low degree of internal cohesiveness in India and Pakistan influence policy-making decisions. India likes to think of itself as being constrained, or alternatively, as having a great asset in its democratic system. Pakistan regularly asserts that it, too, has to account to popular demands and that elected officials should be guided by Islamic mandates. Not infrequently, of course, so-called popular demands are in reality manufactured by policy makers in reality, and made to serve as rationalization for decisions. So, for example, authorities must acknowledge their role in helping to form public opinions that supposedly constrain governments from making concessions in the Kashmir dispute.

External Weights in the Balance

Through nearly all Pakistan's history, its efforts to overcome India's pre-eminence have taken the form of building alliances with other states. The success of Pakistan in attracting external assistance has been partial and never entirely to its satisfaction. The country learned long ago that it could not expect to rely on its nominal allies. The United States, entering the Cold War era, was a willing partner but – like China and the Arab states – could not be counted on to take Pakistan's side automatically on the major issues. Notably, nothing more than moral support from these allies was available for Pakistan during its armed confrontations with India. (Ironically, Pakistan's loss of its East Wing in 1971, while underscoring subnational security problems, left the country better off politically and geostrategically.) Despite the often generous financial rewards and material resources provided, external powers have never succeeded in significantly altering India's advantage in the region's balance of power. Although the superiority of India in conventional military terms has been reduced by outside help in Pakistan's acquisition of nuclear capabilities, the overall imbalance remains – especially the dominance of India as an economic power.

Of course Washington's long-term interest in Pakistan involved containing communism. The effort to acquire strategic partners took on major significance during Zulfikar Ali Bhutto's tenure as Foreign Minister in the Muhammad Ayub government in the 1960s and again during the 1970s when Bhutto was prime minister. Pakistan sought to make the Arab Middle East a serious counterweight against India. Pakistan also sought a regional institutional relationship with Iran and Turkey through the Regional Co-operation for Development (RCD) and initiated serious rapprochement with China. More broadly, Prime Minister Bhutto sought to restore Pakistan's links and credentials with the third world and nonaligned countries.

With the invasion of Afghanistan, Pakistan was able to regain the military aid from the United States that it had lost at the end of the 1970s. The war enabled a regime whose legitimacy was in serious doubt to gain a new lease on life. But a Soviet military presence in Afghanistan and Moscow's now solid alignment with New Delhi revived the nightmare for Pakistan of a pincer movement that would overwhelm the country's defenses. To avoid this threat, General Zia ul-Haq gave explicit blessing to a policy of strategic depth against India, based on strengthening Pakistan's Islamic ties. Pakistan enhanced its reputation among Islamic states when it took the diplomatic lead against the communists in Afghanistan.

By 1985, with the creation of the South Asian Association for Regional Co-operation (SAARC), an institutional framework to further economic cooperation was put in place that might, in time, lead to the reduction of political tensions. But with bilateral issues between member countries ruled off the agenda, opportunities for progress on the interrelated economic and political fronts have been minimal. Pakistan is also a charter member of the Economic Co-operation Organization (ECO), that after the breakup of the Soviet Union came to include all the former Muslim republics, as well as Afghanistan. This expanded organization, which best defines the potential boundaries of strategic depth for Pakistan, was meant to encourage mutually profitable commercial projects and other forms of cooperation for development. It too, however, has run afoul of political and economic incompatibilities.

Pakistan scored its greatest successes in its bilateral relations during the 1980s. By means of astute diplomatic skills, Islamabad was able to sustain friendly relations with Iran, Saudi Arabia and the United States at the same time. More recently, however, Pakistan has shown little of its previous finesse. Indeed, Islamabad finds itself more isolated internationally than at any time in its history. In supporting the Taliban, Pakistan has sacrificed good relations with Iran and much of the rest of the region. Pakistan will pay a particularly heavy price if a Tehran–New Delhi axis emerges – ideology and religion notwithstanding.

The contributions of the United States and the Soviet Union to sustaining the power balance in South Asia changed rather abruptly in the 1990s. This change followed the Soviet withdrawal from Afghanistan, the demise of the Soviet Union, and the rediscovery of Pakistan's nuclear program by the United States. After 1990, India found itself forced to open itself up to the international economy. Moscow, preoccupied with its political and economic instability and desperate for hard currency, was no longer in a position to extend generous credits to the Indian government and sustain a barter trade. The United States stopped playing a direct part in Pakistan's defense strategies and development plans. With US law providing the rationale, foreign aid was halted in 1990, although the flow of assistance did not stop immediately.

In the absence of superpower patrons, many of the strategic choices by Pakistan and India are being made on the basis of independent assessments of their security. The Cold War sometimes provoked countries to act, even against their own best interests, for the good of their military and economic partners. But it also provided discipline that restrained some countries from more imprudent behavior. To the extent that external constraints exist in decision-making today, the global economic system can punish behavior, largely in the form of forfeited credits, trade and investments. With appropriate political sanctions absent, aside from international opinion, and typical international reluctance to apply or sustain economic sanctions, foreign policies in South Asia are able to follow a more nationalist course. This leaves countries in the region more vulnerable to leaders who prey on citizens' emotions and prejudices.

Indian and Pakistani policy makers both complain publicly about a lack of understanding of their countries' legitimate security concerns, especially by the United States. Indians express resentment over what appears to be a bias in Washington favoring Pakistan and China, and many in Pakistan are certain that key decision makers in Washington tilt toward India. In its disappointment with the United States, Pakistan has sought to diversify its sources of economic assistance and has become increasingly dependent on loans from international creditor institutions. Governments in Islamabad value arms transfers from China more than ever, and pleas for financial backing from states in the Gulf have taken on a new significance. However, the current low export prices for oil and the debt that remains from the 1991 Gulf War make it highly unlikely that these states will stage a rescue of Pakistan's badly stumbling economy.

Strategic depth was supposed to be Pakistan's insurance policy. In fact, this concept has never been carefully defined and is as much a psychological as a political or military one. At a minimum, it has meant that Pakistan's military planners could take the country's western borders for granted. This depth was supposed to provide a defensive fallback, with Iran, Afghanistan and the Arab states providing reliable counterweights to a hegemony-seeking India. In fact, there is no likelihood that Iran and the Arab states will give Pakistan the political backing it seeks on the Kashmir issue. The apparent gains in strategic depth with the installation of a friendly regime in Kabul have amounted instead to a net liability.

Iran's threatened military intervention in Afghanistan during the early fall of 1998 seemed finally to have put to rest any remaining notions about strategic depth. In a relationship already strained by years of backing opposing camps in the post-1992 Afghan civil war, Tehran and Islamabad were more estranged than ever. As late as May 1998, Iran had defended Pakistan's nuclear testing and thought that it had a commitment from the Nawaz Sharif government to a common approach to bring together the warring groups in Afghanistan. But Pakistan's visible complicity in the Taliban's largely decisive summer 1998 campaign, together with alleged atrocities against Shia populations across Afghanistan and above all, the murders in Mazar-i-Sharif of Iranian diplomats, induced bitter feelings in Tehran.

Geopolitical thinking also led Pakistan's policy makers to strive for new opportunities to enable their country to escape its subordinate status in South Asia by aspiring, somewhat unrealistically, to commercial, political and cultural leadership of an emerging Central Asia. Pakistan's Afghan policy has prompted Central Asia's Muslim states to join Russia in thrusting themselves into South Asia's power equation. Instead of welcoming Pakistan's overtures, as they did earlier, these former Soviet republics have demonstrated their displeasure with Islamabad's policies by strengthening ties to India. Like Russia, they hold the Pakistan government responsible for the Taliban's success in extending the movement's military grip over most of Afghanistan. The Russians, once willing to play mediator in the region, have again sided solidly with India in their mutual desire to insulate the region from the export of Islamic fundamentalism. India's attempt to rebuild commercial and military links with Russia and the Central Asian republics represents its response to Pakistan's alignment with China. In search of technical and military assistance, India has also made Israel a factor in the South Asian area.

China in the Equation

The South Asian power equation cannot be realistically assessed without taking China into account. Beijing sees itself as an emerging economic, political and military superpower, with real and expanding interests in South and Southeast Asia. As such, China challenges India's pre-eminence, and their relationship has settled into a protracted rivalry. In the absence of a strategic buffer, competing territorial claims have long brought China into India's security planning. Since the mid-1960s, China has lent its political weight and transferred arms to Pakistan in a vain attempt to create a counterweight to Indian hegemony. But Indian policy makers in the 1990s insisted that Chinese aims – directed at securing port facilities and economic dependencies, and generally, in seeking to project its influence over the Indian Ocean – indicated a broader design. As further evidence, they cited arms transfers to Bangladesh, Sri Lanka and Myanmar.

Above all, India believes that the power balance in South Asia is affected by the fact that China is a nuclear power. Indian leaders express concern that China will use its quantitative and qualitative superiority in nuclear weapons to intimidate the subcontinent and control the region's future. Indian policy makers choose to believe that over the long term China will inevitably develop highly aggressive tendencies, pushing ahead vigorously with the development of tactical, strategic and theater nuclear weapons. Without a credible nuclear deterrent, India reasons that it will be vulnerable to blackmail or worse.

But a good case can be made that China's challenge to India is wrongly perceived. India is far more threatened by being left behind economically than by military and political pressures. It is economic competition with China in regional and global markets that will determine the winners and losers in the twenty-first century. China's interest does not seem to be in extending political control beyond its borders but in nailing down and exploiting markets. Whatever the uncertainties arising from a nuclear build-up in India, China may take some comfort from the fact that the expense of India's efforts to catch up militarily could well seal its fate as an economic backwater.

China's primary interest seems to be in sustaining an environment that promotes economic growth and assures domestic control, based on continued political dominance by the Communist party. China's desire is for stability on the borders, for which nothing more adventurous than the shoring up of friendly forces is required. For Chinese leaders to act more threateningly would only make Russia and even the United States more inclined to come to India's defense. Nor is China anxious to have US–Pakistani relations become any closer than they are at present, as might happen if India became more aggressive in response to increased Chinese pressures.

By similar logic, it would not seem to be in China's interest to have Pakistan's nuclear program progress much beyond the minimum requirements. Certainly, it does not want to see Pakistan pose a sufficient threat to goad India into aggressive action. Enough support for a minimal deterrence by Pakistan serves China's aims as well as allays international criticism of Chinese assistance. Should India become very forceful in dealing with Pakistan, Chinese policy is less certain. If the 1971 war is a guide, China will shun direct military involvement. Yet three decades later, the stakes are far higher.

After a 1993 border agreement it seemed that, despite unresolved disputes, Sino–Indian relations had acquired some stability. No serious confrontation between the countries has occurred since 1986–87, and most observers concluded that both countries were trying to effect a rapprochement. Although China's arms build-up has continued, with, for example, including the development of its long range Dongfeng-31 missile, China's nuclear arsenal, whether aimed at India or anyone else, remains at least one step away from direct deployment, whether aimed at India or anyone else. Arguably, in over three decades there has not been any instance in which China has used its nuclear advantage to bully India.

The rationale made by key Indian policy makers for the May 1998 nuclear tests that labeled China as a real and present danger may have only succeeded in arousing a sleeping dragon, creating a self-fulfilling prophecy. Perhaps in recognition of this, the rhetoric from New Delhi softened in subsequent months. Even so, China's leaders are believed to have taken great offense. For relations to improve, India will probably have to tone down demands for equality, which China finds hard to accept whether militarily, economically or even culturally. In turn, China will have to acknowledge India's desire to be viewed as the pre-eminent regional power in South Asia to a greater degree than it has to date. Curiously, although India is usually described as the world's largest democracy and China the largest authoritarian, communist regime, these ideological and institutional differences seem to matter very little in determining how they shape their policies toward one another.

At present, India is resentful about what it views as a firm Washington–Beijing axis that rests essentially on mutual economic interests. Yet some Indian analysts envision a souring of the relationship over the long term, with the emergence of a highly assertive, possibly aggressive China. A convergence of global and regional interests is then expected to drive the United States and India toward an alliance to contain China. This scenario may be largely wishful thinking. But the possibility of increased cooperation between India and the United States is suggested in the tacit support given by India in recent years for a number of American foreign policy initiatives, and by investment policies that have made India attractive to an increasing number of multinational firms. Indian leaders feel that their claim that Pakistan is an important source of instability outside its borders is finally gaining a sympathetic hearing in the United States, notably in the US Congress. Their views seem vindicated by recent events, which they believe help boost their case that Pakistan contributes to terrorism, religious extremism and narcotics trafficking through its policies in Kashmir and Afghanistan.

The Nuclear Balance

The emergence of India and Pakistan as declared nuclear weapons states has made the security environment in South Asia more complex by adding new uncertainties and an increased volatility. While the possibility of conventional armed conflict may be reduced by the fear that hostilities could quickly escalate into a nuclear exchange, the prevailing asymmetries create incentives for preemptive action. Moreover, the consequences of errors in judgment or an accident are infinitely more lethal. Tensions between the two countries have surged with testing, shattering for the present, any hopes of bilateral cooperation in a number of significant areas. They have also aroused the concerns of other states in South Asia.

Because of the proximity of India and Pakistan, both countries would necessarily share consequences of a nuclear exchange; to a high degree, the use of nuclear weapons by either side would be self-destructive. Moreover, should any weapons be detonated, they would have an environmental impact on the entire subcontinent and beyond. An estimated 100 million Indians and Pakistanis might eventually die from the explosions, and the fallout would spread over a wide area, certainly including Bangladesh and much of Southeast Asia, and probably parts of China and Central Asia.

Gaining admission to the nuclear club has subjected India and Pakistan to outside pressures to stem a budding arms race on the subcontinent and adopt procedures and accords that will lessen the likelihood that nuclear weapons will ever be used. Most attention is centered on getting the two countries to adhere to the CTBT and agree to the NPT. On the part of India, the rejection of the NPT follows from its unwillingness to be left out of the great power nuclear club, which it views as discriminatory and favorable to China's ambitions. Pakistan will accede to nothing that India rejects. The case for no further testing and the acceptance of curbs on the production of fissile materials is more compelling, especially since little would be binding, and the nuclear development programs of the two countries are unlikely to be affected. But neither country is likely to sign any treaty without concessions from the West on financial and other issues.

India and Pakistan regularly characterize as patronizing, the concerns expressed in the West that question their ability to manage nuclear weapon systems. But international anxieties appear to have some basis. Neither India nor Pakistan has developed a reliable command and control system or enunciated a reliable nuclear doctrine that would govern use of the weapons. By most calculations, the effects of Mutually Assured Destruction (MAD), along with high levels of intelligence, helped the Cold War superpowers to avoid nuclear war but neither of these are expected developments in the subcontinent in the near future.[4]

The constraints of MAD for the United States and Soviet Union were based on having a variety of delivery systems, including submarine missiles. With India and Pakistan dependent on land-based missiles for the foreseeable future and lacking the kind of surveillance systems available to the superpowers, there is no warning time after a launch to detect a false reading. Thus, decisions by the two may be made precipitously in a crisis and encourage a preemptive attack. Because neither side has a good idea of what the other might be deploying, it becomes necessary to assume the worst. In any case, the risk factors for these two countries – having already fought costly wars in 1947, 1965, 1971 and recently at Kargil – are higher than those of the Cold War era, during which the superpowers had some close calls. India and Pakistan have, of course, a perennial flash point in Kashmir.

Even with a system of crisis management in place and the dangers of accident minimized, there is reasonable concern that the two states, both of which are still at the fledgling stages of nuclear stockpiling, may consider a decision to make preemptive launch to be rational. The danger is more likely to come from Pakistan, which not only has fewer weapons but also is less able to survive an exchange. If Pakistan's military concludes that war is imminent, the temptation exists to call for a first strike, particularly if Pakistan believes that its bombs can destroy most of India's launch pads. Knowing this, Indian strategists may logically conclude that it is safer to preempt the Pakistani attack with one of their own. Thus a hair-trigger environment is created – at least until both sides have gained confidence in deterrence, which India's proposed nuclear doctrine hopes to realize with a triad defense.

As the sixth declared nuclear state, India has furthered few of its strategic objectives. If the objective is to ward off the possibility of future nuclear blackmail from China, it is hard to see how India has made progress. The more it seeks nuclear deterrence against China, the greater the stimulus for China to increase its own expenditure and widen the power differential between the two. Should India decide to move decisively to accumulate a large nuclear stockpile and develop long-range missiles, China could well respond by mounting new military pressures along disputed mountainous territory. It could also substantially increase its arms and technology transfers to Pakistan. Both countries have reason to review their deterrent capabilities against India, should Russian sales of advanced aircraft to India proceed and New Delhi makes a serious effort to build an anti-missile defense system. It is more than a little ironic that India, by its decision to test and revive military cooperation with Russia, promotes Pakistan's security reliance on China, which was one of the reasons that India cited for its new nuclear policy. Such Sino-Pakistani cooperation undermines India's superiority in conventional forces.

Nuclear weapons are also unlikely to prevent Pakistan's more or less clandestine involvement in the rebellion in Indian-held Kashmir and the Punjab. Instead, as a means to avoid taking direct responsibility for actions aimed at destabilizing each other, both countries may be tempted to increase their support for insurgencies. What India wants is for other powers to limit Pakistan's role in Afghanistan and for Pakistan to cease clandestine operations inside India. Authorities in New Delhi predictably fail to mention their own destabilizing activities in Pakistan.

The decision by Pakistan to become the seventh declared nuclear power in the world was heralded by former Prime Minister Nawaz Sharif, as strengthening the country's ability to defend its borders. Supposedly, a strategic parity has been introduced in the region as a result of testing. Pakistan's leaders talk in terms of an "equalizer," which Pakistan has achieved with its nuclear arsenal. However, Pakistan's nuclear tests have not altered the overall military balance in the region. They have only confirmed what was long accepted – that both countries have the capacity to develop nuclear weapons.

Some contend that the disclosure about the programs contributes to stability, but a *de facto* stability previously existed under conditions of ambiguity. Long before May 1998, an all-out war between the countries had become difficult to contemplate. The two countries had managed to avoid a major conflict since the war that created Bangladesh. So long as Pakistan remained at a conventional force disadvantage of roughly three to one, India did not need nuclear weapons to keep Pakistan at bay. At the same time, the prevailing mutual nuclear ambiguity did not constrain either country from pursuing plans for self-defense.

The restraints of recent decades may now have been upset. While testing has not in itself increased the chances of conflict, the expected deployment of nuclear weapons could succeed in altering the status quo. It is hard to argue, as many in India do, that Pakistan's test launching of its Ghauri missile was provocative and forced India to test, because the Pakistani missile program lags behind India's in terms of technology. However, Pakistani tests have probably given a green light to Indian hawks who wish to make their program far more sophisticated, mainly in the area of missile delivery systems.

Both countries may yet conclude that their purposes are served by a credible minimum deterrence. This is the case when there is a capacity for nuclear weapons to inflict destruction sufficient to discourage military adventure by an adversary, but not to realize a decisive victory. Pakistan need not achieve parity with India to have a deterrent. In theory, Pakistan could obtain its deterrent capability with a relatively small number of nuclear weapons. For Pakistan to do more than this would presumably persuade India to establish a major program and drive both sides to engage in extensive production, testing and fail-safe programs. What either country may conceive to be minimum deterrence is likely to change, however, because of continual reassessment regarding the capability needed to provide an insurance policy. But while Pakistan measures its requirement against Indian capability, India calculates what is sufficient by the size of the Chinese arsenal and the need for a credible stockpile of nuclear weapons. As India moves to meet its challenge from China, Pakistan is likely to feel the need to redefine minimum deterrence and raise its own capabilities. As one country tries to trump the other, the threshold of what constitutes sufficient capability constantly rises.

Pakistan's decision makers have argued that they were not offered the kind of security guarantees that might have served as justification for restraint in testing their nuclear weapons. Even so, the Islamabad government forfeited substantial economic dividends promised by Washington, Japan and others. These concessions from a concerned international community would have gone far in helping the country to overcome an approaching budgetary and fiscal crisis and avoided post-testing policies that exacerbated problems of confidence in the economy. Although India is also likely to suffer financially from sanctions, Pakistan has more to lose. Apart from losing bilateral and multilateral aid, both countries will witness a slowdown in the rate of the foreign private investment on which they have pinned much of their hopes for economic growth and international competitiveness. India and Pakistan may be nuclear states, but they are hardly nuclear powers – at least not without a more prosperous industrial economy and a more stable, enlightened society. Certainly, Pakistan's acquisition of nuclear status is not a particularly noteworthy feat, for even the poorest of states can build a nuclear weapon when it is willing to divert scarce resources to the project. This is especially true when, as in the case of Pakistan, the technology has been imported – one way or another.

Domestic pressures in Pakistan may have permitted no alternative to testing after the Indian decision to do so. The lack of trust in the United States and the certainty that opposition parties would try to gain political advantage are generally acknowledged. Yet the considerable majority enjoyed at the time by the Pakistan Muslim League in the National Assembly assured the government a continued grip on power. Had Prime Minister Nawaz Sharif wanted, he could have tried to steer public opinion. To overcome popular sentiment favoring the demonstration of nuclear muscle would, admittedly, have required intelligent, convincing leadership. The challenge became especially hard once New Delhi shamelessly goaded Pakistan to test, and partly remove the international pressures on India, by questioning the ability of Pakistan's scientists to detonate a bomb. But in neither Pakistan nor India did decision makers show any interest in leading a public debate over the costs and benefits of testing. The public was handed a *fait accompli*, after which dissent could only seem unpatriotic. Only subsequently have doubts been raised about the course taken and its consequences, mostly by the independent press in both countries.

In India, some have argued that the decision to develop nuclear weapons runs counter to the country's national ethos and traditions. What could be further from Gandhi's philosophy, they point out, than a life-threatening weapon? However, modern Indian politics poses few philosophical obstacles. Although it took the ultra-nationalist BJP government to take the final step, the feeling that the policy of nuclear ambiguity should be discarded had been building for some time. Nuclear testing had long been part of the BJP's platform and ideology. Moreover, when the ruling party found itself having to compromise with coalition partners over other issues, testing provided an easy way to console party loyalists.

The testing controversy was expected by Pakistan's policy makers to draw international attention to the dispute over Kashmir. There is no evidence however, that international endorsement of Pakistan's position has become stronger or more widespread. At least for the present, the declaration of nuclear status seems to have stiffened the resolve of Indian and Pakistani leaders to press their separate cases. Boasts to their respective peoples about enhanced military capabilities have not prepared them for necessary compromises. Despite the heightened dangers of military escalation, conflict along the cease-fire lines has intensified and the need for nuclear restraint may have actually prompted Pakistan's risk-taking at Kargil.

The international community is likely to have little to show for trying to induce India and Pakistan to turn back the clock on nuclear development. Sanctions alone will not alter the countries' policies and may, in fact, be counter-productive. It is more likely that appropriate incentives are needed if international pressures to halt the process of nuclear weaponization and the export of material technology are to succeed. Where possible, these should involve assistance in creating procedures to manage and control weapons. Help in safeguarding nuclear stockpiles should also include systems to increase the likelihood that informed and prudent decisions will be made. Without these, the nuclear standoff that is emerging, leaves open the danger of accident and mis-calculation from bureaucratic or technical ineptitude.

To date, neither India nor Pakistan seem to have a sufficient sense of urgency about developing the type of stable nuclear relationship that can only be attained through regular discussions and confidence-building measures, even if the final resolution of their differences remains elusive. Little progress can be detected despite expressions of a willingness on both sides to maintain high-level talks, institute a crisis hotline and tone down hostile propaganda. However symbolic an agreement on a bus service between the countries may be, it remains only a token of what remains to be accomplished in terms of building trust. Even if both India and Pakistan end their testing programs, either *de facto* or as a result of a treaty, the arms race in South Asia may continue. Only formal agreements, incorporating monitoring arrangements, can assure each country that the other is not proceeding with its development and stockpiling of more sophisticated nuclear weapons.

Afghanistan in the Balance

The success of the Taliban in Afghanistan's civil war carries its own consequences for the balance of power in the region. In the short term at least, India seems to have suffered a setback in Afghanistan. It has lost what had been, in effect, a second front against Pakistan. Until 1996, governments in Kabul could be depended on to turn eventually to India as a political and economic counterweight to an overbearing Pakistan. This had been the case under the Afghan monarchy, during Sardar Daoud's tenure and the 15 years of communist rule, and even during the shorter-lived government led by Burhanuddin Rabbani. In contrast, the Taliban government is not expected to turn its back on Pakistan by reaching out to India at any time in the foreseeable future. India understandably feels anxious about a regime in Afghanistan that could influence the behavior of Muslims across the region.

Despite the presence of a friendly government in Kabul, however, Pakistan's strategic position in the region has deteriorated considerably. Backing for the Taliban has evoked anger in neighboring countries and condemnation internationally. The loss in terms of relations with Iran far outweighs any gain that Pakistan may have realized by helping to install a government of its liking in Kabul. Iran has been humiliated in Afghanistan by the defeat of its favored militias and its failure to protect the largely Shia, Hazara community. Pakistan is held most directly to blame for the Taliban's lack of political and military restraint.

Defense planners in Pakistan, who could in the past take a peaceful western border for granted, have reason to worry about threats of armed intervention by Tehran against the Taliban, and the possibility of Pakistan being drawn into the conflict. Admittedly, when Iran moved troops to its Afghan frontier in the fall of 1988, direct military involvement by Pakistan was thought highly unlikely. Yet in a protracted war, religious parties and other groups in Pakistan sympathetic to the Afghan cause made it difficult for Islamabad to deny the Taliban moral and political support. *De facto* permission for Afghan fighters and the provision of equipment to cross the Pakistan border would in all probability, have drawn heavy criticism and conceivably led to retaliatory measures by Iran. After all, the dominant view in Tehran remains that the United States, with Pakistan's complicity, has conspired to sustain the Taliban in order to contain Iran and deny it opportunities for economic recovery at home and commercial access and political influence in Central Asia.

The Central Asian governments, together with their Russian sponsor, view the proximity of a fundamentalist Islamic force as inherently destabilizing for the region, and as having the capability to undermine political control and social cohesion through the training of terrorists and trafficking of drugs. In contrast to the wishes of Pakistan, these Muslim republics would prefer a fragmented, unstable Afghanistan to the possibility of the Taliban's consolidation of power. Islamabad's support for a Taliban-dominated country has also complicated Pakistan's relations with China, Pakistan's most steadfast ally. The Beijing government is uneasy about an ascendant Afghan regime that seeks to spread its brand of Islam. Verbally at least, the Taliban have already challenged China's policies in Xinjian province, and Beijing alleges the infiltration of trained agitators. The success of radical Islamic forces in Afghanistan has likewise brought criticism from Ankara, expressed in its sympathy for Iran's anti-Taliban stance. A radicalized Afghanistan is viewed as unhealthy competition for Turkish interests and ambitions in Central Asia.

Pakistan has paid heavily for having admitted millions of Afghan refugees over the course of 20 years, at least a third of whom remain. The introduction of guns and drugs into Pakistan's cities and the social disruption and violence that directly or indirectly can be traced to Afghan refugees will continue to cause problems for many years to come. As a price for having sustained the Taliban military campaigns, Pakistan has also inherited responsibility for the viability of an Afghan state that is virtually without an economy, modern or otherwise. With the Taliban having alienated most of the international agencies and private organizations working in Afghanistan, the costs of relief and rehabilitation are expected to fall heavily on Pakistan, which is itself in dire financial straits. The inadequacy of aid from Pakistan is bound to create resentment among Afghans.

Pakistan has regularly experienced a lack of discipline and gratitude on the part of its proteges in Afghanistan. The conclusion of the Afghan war, with the departure of the Soviets and the defeat of the Afghan communists, did not in fact, bring with it the same influence that Pakistan had exercised over the *Mujahideen* during the 1980s, when their base of operations was in Peshawar, Pakistan. Instead, in the post-communist era, the Islamabad government shifted its support from leader to leader, none of whom were very capable or sufficiently beholden to it. Even among the Taliban, the leaders who have taken Islamabad's logistical advice and material assistance in battle, resist political dictates from their Pakistani allies. When it is a matter of Islamic principle, as they see it, they will not yield. The Taliban's policies on human rights especially, are a political embarrassment for its Pakistani sponsors. In the course of assisting the Taliban economically and militarily, Pakistan has also contributed to deepening sectarian and ethnic divisions in Afghanistan.

Worse still for Pakistan, is the concern that Islamabad's Afghan policies will eventually backfire. Instead of Pakistan modifying the behavior of the Taliban, the leadership in Afghanistan seeks to impose its Islamic agenda inside Pakistan. If they ever achieve complete victory in Afghanistan, the Taliban could shift their attention to Pakistan and drive the country towards becoming a more 'authentic' Islamic state. The Taliban's understanding of the *Ummah* makes national boundaries inconsequential where Islamic mandates are at issue. Kabul's policies could guarantee rising religious militancy and sectarianism in Pakistan, with a consequent threat to the county's political cohesion and stability. The Taliban considers Shias as apostates, and Sunni-Shia strife has been a continuing feature of the Pakistan social scene. Close links exist between the Taliban – mostly ardent Deobandi Sunnis – and like-minded doctrinal groups in Pakistan. The ranks of the Taliban are composed of young Afghans who were brought up in Pakistan and received their *madrassah* education there before joining the movement. Their continuing family connections and business interests also further the Taliban's penetration of Pakistan's society.[5] Furthermore, in recent years large numbers of Pakistanis have trained in Afghanistan for combat in Kashmir – receiving indoctrination along with military skills.

Real Security

Pakistan and India need peace and stability if they are to acquire security in the broadest sense. Yet this security is far more determined by domestic developments than by external ones. As a result of their policies, however, both countries have allowed social conditions to be created that undermine their futures. The danger is embedded in poor educational, health and other social welfare programs that fail to provide the human resources needed to compete globally and also exact a high daily price in human costs. The late Mahbub ul-Haq underscored these issues when he formulated his Human Development Index, a measure of life expectancy, education and welfare that has been published annually since 1990: both Pakistan and India rank near the bottom of the index. In fact, Pakistan is often placed in the category of sub-Saharan African countries because of its human development investment and its statistics on social sector spending.[6]

For Pakistan and India, it comes down to investment priorities. If their economies are to bear the brunt of further increases in defense spending in a nuclear era, their social and development sectors are bound to suffer. Pakistan has little choice. Defense and debt repayments already consume roughly 70 percent of the federal budget. In per capita terms, the country spends US$21 on arms against India's US$10. Pakistan also spends 125 percent more on defense than on health and education combined, while India spends an unacceptably high 65 percent more. As a proportion of its Gross National Product (GNP), Pakistan spends more than twice as much as India on defense.[7] While decision makers in both countries acknowledge that neither can adequately care for its citizens, the greatest sacrifices always seem to be borne by the poorest.

If Pakistan becomes a "failed state," it will not be because of threats at its borders. Pakistan will implode, if it does, because its new military-led government fails to revive citizens' faith in their national institutions and leaders, or reduce the inequities of a feudal society. There is concern that if Pakistan's economy continues to deteriorate, regional and centripetal forces will gain ground, leading toward national disintegration. Pakistan's preoccupation with its security is justified, but its assessment of the origins of its problems is incorrect. Until this misconception is rectified, it is unlikely that the country will learn to address effectively the very real risks that it faces.[8]

If the powers in the region, including China, are to be able to manage their differences, they need at a minimum, to reach consensus on what constitutes real security and how their interests intersect and overlap. There is a need, for example, to appreciate the significance of progress in technology transfers. There is also a need to understand the positive potential of regional trade. Bilateral and regional cooperation can serve as a powerful incentive for developing normal relationships. India and Pakistan have considerable potential as political and economic leaders in the subcontinent and throughout Asia. The most meaningful competition among the region's states is over access to markets and foreign investment. The outcome of this economic competition has bearing, of course, on relative military and political standing. Along with social sector achievements, the various measures of national well-being are interrelated and deeply interdependent.

The failure of Pakistan and India to reach a *modus vivendi* has left all of South Asia unfulfilled in terms of realizing its political and economic potential. The future of the region is held hostage to a security environment in which neither India nor Pakistan seems able to discard the past or establish a vision for the future that is based on valid assessments of its security deficiencies. To date, there are few grounds to be optimistic that integrative policies will replace confrontational ones. Leaders in neither country have moved beyond their mutual threat or been able to acknowledge that their societies are at greater risk than their states. Until India and Pakistan are better able to put aside mutual misconceptions and enter into sustained dialogue, they are unlikely to appreciably improve the well-being of their citizens or offer greater assurance against the possibility of nuclear tragedy.

Conclusion

The structural relationship between India and Pakistan seems unlikely to change in the near future, despite recent nuclear proliferation in the subcontinent. Armed and deployed weapons will affect the threat calculations used by the two countries, possibly setting limits on conventional war but raising the stakes in any armed confrontation. Yet there is no indication that India and Pakistan are ready to alter the way they interact – currently manifested in *realpolitik*-based strategies. This seems especially regrettable since potential nuclear dangers should logically accelerate interaction, if not cooperation. The countries' newly acquired, albeit small, nuclear arsenals should prompt the realization that the management of their differences is more urgent than ever before.

For changes to occur in national policies there must be more serious domestic dialogue about national priorities, both within elite policy circles and the public sphere. The absence of a public forum is, of course, in part understandable in light of the normally secretive nature of decision-making on nuclear strategy. However, broader social issues are involved in the choice of whether to develop nuclear weapons and missile capabilities. A public dialogue should also lead governments to treat nuclear policies more systematically, according to how they affect regional and international interests.

One hope for fostering a greater exchange between India and Pakistan lies in a future mutual realization of democracy. Although the proposition that democracies do not fight each other has some validity, the evidence comes mostly from experiences in developed Western countries. It is far too early to claim that this thesis also holds true for developing countries. Moreover, the character of democracy in South Asia, and until recently in Pakistan, leads many to debate the essential character and basis of democracy. Both countries face strains from ethnic, sectarian and sub-regional forces. India's traditional secular system is challenged by Hindu radicalism, while the discontinuity in Pakistan's democratic experience is again manifest in its October 1999 coup.

The dangerous relationships of South Asia are unlikely to be managed without the resolution of major outstanding issues. In the absence of any agreement, the possibility of sudden escalation in tensions and mistakes in judgment are not only possible, but probable. Change in India and Pakistan requires both progress in settling Kashmir's future and a willingness to forego attempts to incite each other's ethnic and sectarian minorities. At the same time, a reconciliation in Indo–Pakistani relations may not be possible without the mediation of trusted external parties, possibly close neighbors who are neutral powers. Very little in the history of the relationship between the two countries suggests that, left to themselves, they can work out their disagreements unassisted. Third parties have on occasion been successful in helping India and Pakistan to reach compromises. Of course, would-be international brokers can facilitate agreements only when the parties to a dispute are in fact looking for mediation. India, as the status quo power, has little incentive to invite outside involvement in the Kashmir issue, and neither country seems ready to accept any advice that would require a change in deeply imbedded perceptions.

Returning to an earlier argument, India and Pakistan remain mired in balance of power strategy that is counterproductive much of the time to the realization of valid national interests in a post-Cold War setting. The two countries still struggle with identity issues and perceived threats to state sovereignty. But India and Pakistan are not exceptions, but represent a sizable, if diminishing number of states whose nationalist ethos governs much of their foreign policy. In contrast stand those states, comprising a growing number of advanced industrial societies, that are in transition to a world in which security is increasingly sought through cooperative international arrangements.[9] These states are likely to prefer openness and candor, and permit mutual involvement, even interference.

Usually labeled as postmodern, they tend to eschew balance of power as a means to contain threats and are unlikely to contest territory. In place of force, they value multilateral constraints that head off conflict. Recognizing their mutual vulnerability, these states are particularly sensitive about nuclear issues and strive to build international regimes that provide safeguards and limit access to critical nuclear technology and materials.

The two classes of countries, the traditional nationalist and the incipient post-modern, find areas of incompatibility in many of their policies. The probability of misunderstanding and disappointment is heightened when they both possess nuclear weapon status. A *realpolitik*-driven foreign policy together with a nuclear capacity is a potentially dangerous combination. Countries like India and Pakistan, which are preoccupied by perceptions of mutual threat, lack the mechanisms and trust needed to reconcile differences. Nationalist-driven geopolitics too often substitutes tired ideologies for constructive policies. The adversarial relationship that India and Pakistan find so difficult to discard, not only threatens the peace of South Asia as a whole, but also challenges many of the assumptions underlying an emerging international order.

2

Nuclearization and Regional Security: An Indian Perspective*

Jasjit Singh

Any examination of the balance of power in South Asia must address three issues. First, in some respects, the very concept of balance of power in South Asia is untenable. The cultural roots of the region and its civilization are based on a deep belief in the oneness of the world rather than its division into competing powers trying to balance each other. In the traditional Indian (subcontinental) culture, use of force is perceived as the instrument of last resort in statecraft, to be used only in defense. This philosophy does not promote any concept or practice of a balance of power amongst states. The question is whether this belief, though true of ancient India and its political philosophy, is applicable in the modern age? The concept of "balance of power," as it is understood in the modern era, is derived primarily from the experience of nineteenth-century Europe. South Asia simply cannot be compared with that model.

Second, serious problems and distortions start to impinge on objective understanding and perceptions if South Asia is considered as an isolated region or if the balance of power there is understood in a geostrategic or geoeconomic vacuum. The continuing conflict in Afghanistan, the East Asian financial crisis, the future of energy security in Asia, a nuclear weapons environment and ballistic missile deployment, two of the world's three largest narcotics producing areas, strategic uncertainties associated with China in the future and a host of other factors necessitate a broader approach to strategic issues than that which the framework of South Asia provides. South Asia is a sub-region deeply influenced not only by historical problems but also by the substantial

---

* The views expressed in this chapter are those of the author and do not necessarily represent the opinions or policies of any organization.

[35]

asymmetry in all elements of what traditionally defines national power and the capabilities of the countries in this sub-region. None of the countries of South Asia have common borders except bilaterally with India. The region has a cultural and civilizational unity, but has for more than five decades consisted of sovereign states that have distinct ideologies and politico-economic interests.

Any objective examination of security issues affecting the countries of South Asia, therefore, needs to take into account a broader framework of political and economic trends, in the global context, as well as developments in the broader region of Asia. While for other countries, especially Pakistan, India may represent the central locus of security issues, for India the concerns extend beyond the subcontinent. For example, nearly 7,000 km of India's 16,000-km land boundary (and 80 percent of its maritime frontier) borders countries not normally included in any definition of South Asia. China is the factor in Indian security calculations that dominates any other possible challenges of the future. China's power has been growing in all respects for the past two decades. It is modernizing its conventional and nuclear military forces and has shown worrisome assertiveness in its foreign policy, especially in recent years. For example, it threatened the United States with nuclear weapons for the first time in 1995–96, over the Taiwan issue. China has a clearly articulated goal of reunification in which the military would bear significant responsibilities. At this stage, it is not clear if China has a reunification agenda beyond Taiwan. For India, it would be imprudent, to say the least, to ignore China's capabilities and its stated goals. China claims a large portion of India in the northeast, and continues to occupy another large segment in the northwest.[1] These claims involve disputed sovereignty and are rooted in the past. It has not been possible to arrive at any acceptable solution to these disputes in spite of persistent efforts over the decades. The lack of transparency in Chinese policies adds to the severe uncertainties about China's future activities.

India's interests require close cooperation with China, if not friendly relations with the country. This has been India's core policy since the very establishment of the People's Republic of China. But India has to cater for any possible failure in attempts to establish close relations. This was the lesson of the 1950s and 1960s, when adequate insurance against such reversal was not created. China and India signed a series of agreements in the 1990s to establish peace and tranquility based on the principle of "mutual and equal security". Such a goal would be a mirage if the actual capabilities to fulfill such a goal were not present. For example, the principle of equal security would not be tenable if one country had nuclear weapons and the other did not. For India, therefore, it is important from a security perspective that nuclear weapons be abolished. (China is not likely to give up its weapons unless other nuclear weapon states do the same). The increasing realization that the world is less interested in total disarmament than mere non-proliferation led India to exercise the nuclear option. For India, nuclear weapons capability continues to be an insurance policy against the possibility of an adverse situation in the future. India was more than satisfied simply to keep the nuclear option open and continue the policy of restraint that it had exercised for nearly four decades. However, the tightening hold of the non-proliferation policies that the dominant powers of the world have pursued in the 1990s while completely ignoring disarmament has led to a change in this policy of restraint. India's nuclear capability is now overt, though a defensive, no-first-use posture is still maintained.

Unfortunately, this fundamental reality about India's own security concerns is not adequately understood in South Asia. Instead, the broad picture drawn is that of Indian 'hegemonic ambitions' in the region. Any such potential for hegemonic assumptions will be greater if the region is defined in the narrower sense as limited to South Asia in which India looms large because of its sheer size. It is forgotten that even in its weakest moment (in December 1962 as a defeated and demoralized nation) India was still the pre-eminent power in South Asia. But what is often lost in such rhetoric is the fundamental fact that there are powers stronger than India whose policies impact on its security, and that India's own interests lie in sustaining peace and stability in the region. The stability, integrity and prosperity of other countries of South Asia, therefore, remain of great importance to India.

Third, the asymmetry of capabilities, assets and liabilities of different states of South Asia are too great to provide even a semblance of a balance among them. The largest state in this sub-region is India, and it has nearly eight times the capabilities (in GDP, size etc.) of Pakistan, the next largest country. This undoubtedly weighs heavily on the politico-strategic consciousness of other countries of the subcontinent.

The Asian Balance of Power

Fundamental changes have been taking place in the nature and direction of the international order which affect the regional situation. While the international order is still in transition, its contours clearly indicate a more polycentric nature which has been accentuated by the collapse of the bipolar structure of the Cold War. While some believed that after the collapse of USSR, the world had become unipolar (or that there was at least a unipolar moment), in reality the international order has been and continues to be *polycentric*, based on the leading role of an expanding constellation of centers of power.[2]

The demise of bipolarity strengthened the emergence of the polycentric world order, which is also progressively shifting the locus of geopolitics. The international order is increasingly becoming Asia-centered and the development and interaction between the centers of power in (geographical) Asia and its proximate territories (rather than an "Asia-Pacific" as propagated by conventional wisdom) are likely to drive the course of politico-economic events. This marks a historic shift from the Euro-centered international order that has dominated the world for two centuries.

The primary centers of power in the emerging international order, with the exception of the European Union, are all in Asia.[3] The half dozen leading centers of power (in its broadest term) and capability include the United States, Japan, China, the European Union (with Germany at its core), Russia and India. Other centers of power are seeking to establish themselves through cooperative mechanisms (such as the Association of Southeast Asian Nations (ASEAN), the Organization of the Islamic Conference (OIC) etc.). According to some estimates, by the year 2015 five out of the seven largest economies in the world will be in Asia, namely, Japan, China, India, Indonesia and Korea. These countries will also contain over 40 percent of the world's population and have a concomitant base of scientific and technological expertise. Russia will have recovered from its economic and political crises by that time. The fastest economic growth rates are in the countries of continental Asia, and so are the most demanding socio-political challenges. The Central Asian and Gulf regions already occupy a critical place in geopolitics because of the energy resources that they hold, and the emerging energy demands at the turn of the century. The interminable war in Afghanistan is largely related to the nature of this new "Great Game".

In fact, the greatest increase in demand for energy in the next century is going to be in what may be called the energy demand heartland: the region containing China, India and South/Southeast Asia. The energy resource base, on the other hand, lies in the periphery of this demand heartland, extending from Asian Russia to Central Asia and from the Gulf to the South and East China Seas. These and other factors alone would suggest that, contrary to conventional wisdom, geographical Asia (rather than the more popular expression 'Asia-Pacific') will be the center of gravity of the international system. The Pacific comes into play because of the United States and its involvement in Asia. Since military power has to operate within the geopolitical and techno-economic context, the emerging world order defines the parameters of the strategic framework for policy makers.

This polycentric order has a number of characteristics. There is a marked asymmetry of power and capability between the leading centers of power. This has imposed concurrent cooperation and competition between them as well as with outside powers. International and strategic relations, especially among the leading centers of power are likely to be issue-based and driven by current national interests. This is best demonstrated by the closer trade relationship between the United States and India, and by the serious differences in their strategic policies, especially concerning proliferation issues. The geopolitical situation of the world will continue to be marked by many uncertainties at least through the early years of the coming decades.

There is a risk that the international arena will become polarized in the future. This could also, theoretically at least, take the form of bipolarity at some future date, although one or both the poles are likely to be different from those in the second half of the twentieth century. From an Indian perspective, a durable non-hegemonic polycentric international order would provide greater scope and an opportunity for cooperative peace. This, in turn, would give greater impetus to human development and prosperity without the negative pressures associated with hegemonies and conflicts. The question that needs to be addressed today is how to sustain and strengthen polycentricity during the twenty-first century in order to provide a cooperative balance of power and avoid any tendency toward polarization. The nature of the geopolitical architecture in Asia will largely determine the shape of the broader international order. The basic issues will be governed by economic and political factors. But nuclear weapons are likely to play their own role, as they did during the Cold War, so long as the international community does not effectively abolish them.

Rationally speaking, nuclear weapons should not be allowed to play a role in international relations. But the reality is that as long as they exist they will continue to have a major impact on perceptions and therefore on the nature of such relations. The argument that nuclear weapons were needed during the Cold War, if it had any validity, lost its justification after the collapse of the Soviet Union. But the nuclear weapon states, instead of moving unambiguously towards the elimination of such weapons, sought to preserve the existing nuclear apartheid in the mean time. China, the major emerging power in Asia, claims that its acquisition of nuclear weapons was necessitated by the Cold War. If this was the central reason, then China should have dismantled its arsenal after the Cold War ended. But the unfortunate reality is that China started to modernize its nuclear arsenal as the Cold War started to wind down. Currently, 96 percent of its nuclear arsenal has relevance only for countries on its borders. As the Cold War ended, and the two super powers indicated their willingness to institute substantive reductions in their nuclear arsenals, China began to recoil from its earlier position that it would join the process of arms reduction when the super powers reduced theirs by 50 percent. Now that the United States and Russia are committed to scale down their nuclear arsenals to less than 30 percent of their holdings in the early 1980s, China wants them to first reduce to the level of its own arsenal before it will embark on any arms reduction dialogue. With its doctrine moving from minimum to limited deterrence, China appears to have started to rely more on nuclear weapons in its strategic policy than ever before.

In 1995–96, China held out a nuclear weapon threat (to the United States) for the first time, following it up for the purposes of coercive diplomacy, with demonstrations of long-range strike capabilities across the Taiwan Straits in March 1996. In December 1995, Lt. General Xiong Guangki, Deputy Chief-of-Staff of the People's Liberation Army, bluntly told a prominent American visitor (former Assistant Secretary of Defense, Charles W. Freeman Jr.) that Beijing would not be intimidated by US threats of intervention on the Taiwan issue, because in the end American leaders "care a lot more about Los Angeles than they do about

Taiwan."[4] Even without provocation, senior Chinese military officers have been saying that the west coast of America is within range of Chinese nuclear weapons – implying also that most of Asia is covered.

By signing a bilateral 'no-first-use' nuclear weapons agreement with Russia, China expects to cover its northern flank. At the same time, the United States plans to deploy ballistic missile defenses in Asia. China has been expressing its concerns on this issue. Following the launch of a rocket by North Korea across Japan, on August 31, 1998, the pressure for deployment of ballistic missile defense will increase. China is likely to respond with counter-measures that will increase its reliance on nuclear weapons and may further encourage it to transfer nuclear and ballistic missile technology to other countries in Asia. Given the facts that Russia has reversed the support that the USSR gave to the abolition of nuclear weapons, and that only China among the five permanent members of the UN Security Council has been advocating their elimination, the prospects of a world free of nuclear weapons are likely to diminish further. It is conceivable, therefore, that given the uncompromising position of the other four nuclear weapon states, nuclear weapons will remain a factor in international relations well into the future.

The evolution of China is loaded with strategic uncertainties. China's power is growing rapidly, and it has made its ambitions to be a superpower explicit. It has an extensive program for the modernization of its military forces, and it has a firmly articulated policy of reunification with Taiwan that does not rule out the use of force and fails to clarify whether there is an agenda of reunification beyond Taiwan. More than 40 years after the Chinese prime minister told Indian Prime Minister Jawaharlal Nehru that its official maps were imperial ones and under revision, these maps continue to indicate China's national boundaries as being south of the Himalayas and including over 94,000 sq. km. of Indian territory. It is realistic to assume that China's pledge not to be the first to use nuclear weapons against another country does not extend to territories (like Aksai Chin and Arunachal Pradesh) that it claims as its own.

It is also in this context that the US approach to China (and Asia) becomes important. US policies tend to undermine the capabilities of some countries, such as India, to ensure a more equitable polycentric balance in Asia. US–China interaction is likely to become the central strategic factor in the world in general, and in Asia in particular. Any polarization caused by the policies of either country will lead to difficult choices for others and also risks expediting polarization of the international order, with far-reaching consequences for the future. The worst-case scenario, of course, would be a return to a bipolar confrontation reminiscent of the recently ended Cold War. Some people believe that an incipient Cold War has already begun on this basis.

China sees the redefined and strengthened US–Japan security alliance (constructed against the USSR, which dissolved seven years ago) as directed against it; while the expansion of the North Atlantic Treaty Organization (NATO), especially if it includes Russia at a future date, appears to China as another step in its containment (and to others as signs of formalizing a Vancouver-to-Vladivostok security system, with the inevitable effect of creating a North–South divide, especially if China is co-opted into this framework). China and Russia have embarked on a path of strategic partnership reminiscent of the 1950s in order to increase their leverage in dealing with the United States. India did not respond to their calls to join the anti-hegemonic coalition. The US appears to find it difficult to adjust to the fundamental changes taking place in the world, and seems to be trying to manage an Asian balance of power by acting as the sole balancer. For Asia, the question remains whether this is the best approach to managing the future and whether this approach will succeed.

Serious concerns were created by US efforts in June 1998 to co-opt China into managing South Asia, giving Beijing a mandate for a sphere of influence in Asia, without even consulting major countries such as India. The clearest illustration of this is US President Bill Clinton's visit to China in June 1998 and related pronouncements. Not only did the content of these statements upset most Indians, they also left another major Asian power, Japan, bewildered. With a vacillating US policy, Japan may have to seek a more independent role if it is to preserve its own interests. This process will be accelerated if North Korea either acquires nuclear weapons or collapses.

Achieving a cooperative balance of power, in contrast to a polarized balance of power built on military force and nuclear weapons in Asia, will require a balance in the relationships between the major countries of the region – that is, Russia, China, Japan, India and the United States – along with cooperative engagement with the European Union on one side and ASEAN and other sub-regional groupings, such as the Gulf Co-operation Council (GCC), on the other. However, this equilibrium would be ephemeral if any one of the major partners in the process is weak. Unfortunately, while India sought to proceed with great restraint and responsibility in its nuclear policy, it was the United States and Western democracies that acted vigorously to undermine India's ability to be self-reliant in its security policy.

Preoccupied as it has been with itself and with its ambition to manage the world, the United States has displayed a fundamental bankruptcy of strategic thought in this regard. In its single-minded drive to "cap, reduce and eliminate"[5] India's nuclear capabilities in the 1990s, one wonders how far the United States considered the geostrategic implications of the success of its own policies. It appears to have ignored the fact that a non-aligned India felt constrained to include a security clause in its 1971 treaty with the Soviet Union in order to provide a political deterrent to possible Chinese intervention in Bangladesh's fight for its independence. The irony that it was finally the United States that sought to intervene, with a nuclear-armed naval task force, in December 1971, appears to have been forgotten over the years. But for India, it has continued to be an abject lesson in *realpolitik*.

The myopic US perceptions of geopolitical realities in Asia are also visible in its attempts to obtain China's cooperation in managing South Asia and India (with Pakistan as a *de facto* strategic ally of both the United States and China). It is in this context that a nuclear India, which for half a century has taken an independent and non-aligned position, is a strategic equalizer and a partner in strengthening non-hegemonic polycentricity.

Nuclear Weapons and Regional Security

With regard to nuclear weapons in the narrower South Asia context, the basic facts have been clouded by the attention paid to the nuclear tests in May 1998. The reality that Pakistan had acquired a credible nuclear weapon deterrent by 1987 was repeatedly claimed by responsible Pakistanis, acknowledged by international observers and factored into Indian security thinking and planning. The United States had even invoked its national laws to cut off military assistance to Pakistan in 1990 because of this. India had tested a nuclear device in 1974, albeit for peaceful purposes, and it had considered carrying out nuclear tests in 1983 and again in 1995. There is little new in the developments of May 1998, except that the official declaration of nuclear weapons acquisition now carries even greater credibility internationally. In examining the implications of the nuclearization of the two countries, five aspects need to be noted.

First, Pakistan's rationale for nuclear weapons acquisition is that India has them, but India's motivations relate to Pakistan only peripherally. This was acknowledged even by the US Secretary of Defense, Dr. William Perry, in a public statement after a visit to the subcontinent in January 1995.[6] The tests and declaration of nuclear weapon status by India and Pakistan do not alter the basic fact that both had credible deterrent nuclear capabilities for many years. The events of May 1998 have only formalized an existing situation.

India's nuclear policy altered course after China acquired nuclear weapons in 1964. Since then, disarmament became an even more important goal for India. But, as importantly, after the search for nuclear security guarantees from the US and the Union of Soviet Socialist Republics (USSR) had failed, a policy of keeping the nuclear option open was adopted.[7] This implied that the option could be closed on the side of non-nuclearization if the world moved toward nuclear disarmament. But it also implied that the option could be closed by acquiring nuclear weapons. In any case, a well-planned nuclear science and technology base was being developed progressively for peaceful purposes. To this was added the challenge of US-led non-proliferation policies that targeted India's open option (while Israel's weapon status went unquestioned).

India's preferred policy was to keep the nuclear option open as long as it was feasible to do so, not to develop nuclear weapons and to work for disarmament, which would eliminate the roots of the nuclear security dilemma. This option of restraint was mostly ignored or not understood in the Western world and it was seen more as a policy of weakness. In fact, it represented an optimum position that minimized costs and maximized capabilities. But states with nuclear weapons, partly to protect their own armed status, set out on the path of non-proliferation with renewed vigor, seeking to roll back India's nuclear program. The basic logic of the renewed focus on non-proliferation may have been general, with selective targeting of 'rogue states', but India was also specifically targeted – although the international community politely refrained from referring to India as a "rogue state." President Clinton's non-proliferation mantra of "cap, reduce, eliminate" nuclear capabilities in South Asia actually targeted India alone, while successive governments of the United States have acquiesced in Pakistan's clandestine nuclear weapons program since 1981 at least. Eminent and knowledgeable Pakistanis claim that since then, a mutual understanding has existed between the United States and Pakistan, to the effect that the former will not hinder the latter's nuclear weapons program in return for Pakistan's willingness to be a front-line state against the Soviet Union in Afghanistan.[8] While approving military-economic aid in 1981, the US Congress added some revealing conditions. It specified that the aid would be suspended ". . . if it [Pakistan] transfers a nuclear explosive device to any non-nuclear state or receives a nuclear device from any country or detonates such a device."[9] So acquiring nuclear expertise from another country or making its own bomb would not hinder US military-economic assistance. Legislation passed in 1995 plugged this loophole, but a way out was found quickly through the Pressler Amendment, which continued US assistance without any hurdle, up to the point at which Pakistan actually possessed a weapon. It is also not surprising in this context that the United States further legitimized Pakistan's clandestine nuclear weapons program when it re-established military supplies to the country, under the Brown Amendment in 1996. These weapons had been embargoed because US laws did not allow their delivery after the US President (as required by law) was unable to certify in 1990 that Pakistan did not have a nuclear bomb.

Very clearly, the wording of the legislation approved by the US Congress ensured that some non-proliferation goals would be pursued, by forbidding the transfer of nuclear devices to and from Pakistan. But it legitimized Pakistan's own program and access to nuclear weapons technology from other countries and assured that the United States would not take any negative action as long as Pakistan did not import or export a nuclear weapon or carry out a test. Even in 1997, the objective of obtaining assurances from China regarding non-transfer of nuclear and missile technology in the future was with respect to Iran, and Pakistan was conveniently left out of the formulation, in spite of credible reports from US senior government officials that China had transferred nuclear weapons technology, including 5,000 ring magnets in 1995 for enrichment of weapons-grade uranium. As it stands, Pakistan has pursued a policy based on the premise that it will do whatever India does. Thus President Clinton's policy actually amounts to "cap, reduce and eliminate" India's nuclear capabilities since Pakistan, by the logic of its own stated positions, would follow suit. The intense pressure brought to bear on India after 1991, though it had not pursued proliferation, unlike some European states, was based on the same logic.

Over the years, evidence has emerged of significant transfers of nuclear weapon technology to Pakistan from the West as well as from China. A 1998 Majority Report of the US Senate Committee stated: "China is the principal supplier of weapons of mass destruction and missile technology to the world, and US government efforts to turn Beijing against international proliferation have met with little success."[10] The difference has been that while the flow from the West has been more in the nature of illegal transactions by private firms, the transfers from China were under the terms of bilateral agreements between the two governments. But there was no ban on a weapon being tested in another country. The late Zulfikar Ali Bhutto had claimed that he had signed the crucial agreement with China in 1976. In 1983, the US Central Intelligence Agency reported that China had provided Pakistan with the design for a nuclear bomb, along with weapons-grade material for two nuclear weapons. China and Pakistan concluded a comprehensive nuclear cooperation agreement in 1986. In 1987, Pakistan acquired tritium purification and production facilities from Germany. According to the Non-Proliferation Studies Center at the Monterey Institute for International Studies, China transferred enough tritium gas to Pakistan for 10 nuclear weapons and "allegedly involved Pakistani scientists in a nuclear test at its Lop Nor site in 1989."

The second factor to be considered in examining nuclearization implications is that Indian and Pakistani rationale for acquiring nuclear weapons are different. Pakistan has sought nuclear weapons essentially to neutralize India's conventional military superiority, which, according to an eminent Pakistani, hangs over Pakistan like a permanent Sword of Damocles.[11] Responsible people in Pakistan have been saying that its acquisition of nuclear weapons has kept the peace in South Asia since 1987, in spite of serious tensions between the two countries.[12] India, on the other hand, sees its necessity for nuclear weapons in relation to the larger framework of an inequitable international order that is made more unequal by the ownership of nuclear weapons by a few, when the answer really lies in global abolition of nuclear weapons. Within this larger issue lies that of national security, which can only be addressed by either global nuclear disarmament or by India's acquisition of nuclear weapons. The need for strategic stability in Asia that involves all nuclear weapon states remains an important objective. Towards this end, India has adopted a doctrine of credible minimum deterrence and declared that it will not be the first to use nuclear weapons and by the same logic, will not use them against a non-nuclear weapon state. Greater clarity in India and Pakistan's nuclear posture would make it possible to institute measures to reduce the risk of accidents or miscalculations.

The third factor is that conventional wisdom would have us focus on the three wars between India and Pakistan since 1947, while ignoring the reality that the two countries have not been at war for 27 years – the longest period in history during which the armies of the subcontinent have not engaged in conflict. The existence of nuclear weapons capabilities in recent years has added to the inhibitions against war. This is so in spite of the fact that relations between the two countries have continued to be frozen at best and tense even in normal times. Relations have been particularly strained since the mid-1980s, when Pakistan started to distance itself from the Simla Agreement of 1972 that laid down the basis of bilateral relations between the two countries. By that time, Pakistan had also started its unconventional war through militancy and terrorism in India. Pakistan's strategy of using military power had relied heavily on the use of irregular warfare preceding the regular conflict. This was so both in 1947–48 and in 1965. So the pursuit of an irregular, proxy war in India's Punjab, followed by a more serious campaign in Jammu and Kashmir, created concerns regarding the possibility of direct invasion. India exercised great restraint, particularly in 1990, to prevent the eruption of war although a great tragedy was being visited on its people as a result of transnational militancy.[13] Militancy in Punjab, where small arms were used extensively, resulted in 21,476 deaths from March 1981 to April 1993. Nearly 38 percent of the people killed in Punjab were militants.

Between 1988 and 1992, more than 26 percent of the 2,424 Kalashnikov assault rifles captured from militants in Punjab were intercepted at the Indo-Pakistani border. Between 1989 and 1992, Indian security forces apprehended 45,640 people in the act of crossing the international border illegally and another 969 people were killed as a result of armed resistance to the security forces during the process of infiltration/exfiltration. More than 97 percent of the incidents of armed violence in Punjab took place in the three districts of Gurdaspur, Amritsar and Ferozepur, west of the Beas river bordering Pakistan; this area also represents the strategic route into Jammu and Kashmir.[14]

While the violence in Punjab was considered appalling, it appears to have been mild, compared with what immediately followed in Jammu and Kashmir. Armed militancy began there on July 31, 1988. A total of 69,975 weapons, 2.85 million rounds of ammunition, 17.2 tons of high explosives and sophisticated equipment, such as 1,671 wireless transmitter sets, were recovered from the militants from March 1988 until March 1998. The Kashmir valley is surrounded by high Himalayan mountains and access to the state is possible only from China, from Pakistan or from within India. There is no evidence that any weapons came directly from China, and it would be ridiculous even to suggest that they were supplied by India. The geography itself and the weight of hard evidence points to large quantities of automatic and highly lethal weapons reaching the border states of India from Pakistan.

Notwithstanding this level of violence through unconventional war, senior military leaders of Pakistan emphasize, as noted earlier, that the subcontinent has been without war for more than a quarter century, in spite of serious tension during the past 15 years. It is possible to argue that nuclear weapons, which it is claimed, have kept the peace in Europe for five decades, would also usher in a prolonged period of peace, or at least a no-war situation in South Asia. In any event, it is clear that even if war breaks out in South Asia or its borders, it will be severely limited by the existence of nuclear weapons. It is true to say that even the earlier wars in South Asia were limited in scope and magnitude, although by choice. Future wars however, will be limited by constraints imposed by the existence of nuclear weapons. On the other hand, while conventional war has been made less likely by the development of nuclear deterrents by China, Pakistan and India, concerns about unconventional war and transnational militancy/terrorism remain. This in fact, has been the dominant pattern for the past decade since Pakistan acquired nuclear weapons. The question is whether a more overt nuclear status will reduce these concerns or escalate them. The answer will define the future prospects of peace and security in South Asia.

The fourth factor to be considered is that, while popular perception would have us believe that Pakistan's acquisition of missiles and nuclear capability is wholly dictated by the India factor, there is a need to focus on other dimensions. These are symbolized by the terminology of "strategic depth", "strategic defiance" and "strategic vision", which gained ground in Pakistan toward the end of the 1980s, almost concurrently with the acquisition of nuclear weapons. The implications of Pakistan's declared nuclear weapons capability and its intermediate-range ballistic missiles remain somewhat uncertain at this stage, for the Islamic world in general and the West Asian region in particular, although these are driven more by the policies of the Arab states than by Pakistan.

There were references to the "Islamic Bomb" and celebrations in many parts of the Arab world after the Pakistani test. But at a more empirical level the question of why Pakistan requires ballistic missiles, such as the Ghauri and Ghaznavi, with ranges of 1,500 to 2,500 kilometers needs to be asked. These will no doubt extend the reach of Pakistani missile strikes over Indian territory. But with the extensive military and economic assets and large population centers of India, including its capital, located within 25–500 kilometers of Pakistan, the investment in longer-range missiles would appear to be infructuous in dealing with India. But they assume a logic of their own, considering that their reach extends over the Gulf region right up to Israel. Seen in the context of Pakistan's ambitions to be the leader of the Islamic world, the drive to acquire long-range missiles while in possession of nuclear weapons begins to acquire a different meaning. While the implications of testing and acquiring the Ghauri missile may be complex, it is certain to provide an impetus to the Indian missile program, which had slowed significantly in recent years.

The fifth factor is that Pakistan's economic condition had been deteriorating for nearly a decade and was in a fairly precarious state when it opted to test. While India will undoubtedly withstand the negative effects of economic sanctions, Pakistan is far more vulnerable in this regard. The impact has already started to reverberate through its fragile political situation and ongoing ethno-sectarian tensions and conflicts. Any shift toward greater instability will have far-reaching and possibly unpredictable consequences for peace and security in South Asia and beyond. India's interests lie in the integrity, stability and prosperity of Pakistan. It is reasonable to expect that Pakistan, with the support of other countries, will be able to stabilize its macro-economic situation. But what is not clear is whether it can reverse the ethno-sectarian conflict raging within its borders, or start to build institutions that have not been developed since the country's creation. GCC countries could play a crucial role in helping Pakistan overcome its present crises.

This leads us to the last but not least important question of the implications of overt nuclearization of India and Pakistan for the countries of West Asia.

There are concerns that the nuclearization of India and Pakistan could provide motivation for the acquisition of nuclear weapons by other countries, especially in Asia. At this stage it is not clear what direction this might take. As noted earlier, India opted for overt nuclear weapons status because of three concurrent factors:

- the absence of progress on nuclear disarmament
- the continuing existence of a potential nuclear weapons threat and hence the need for an insurance against the resultant uncertainty
- a tightening global non-proliferation order that threatened to erode India's option and capability to possess a nuclear deterrent at a future date.

Pakistan sought nuclear weapons to counter a superior conventional military capability that is likely to persist into the indefinite future. All these arguments for nuclearization could be applied to a large number of countries in the region and Asia. But the crucial difference is that, barring the five nuclear weapon states, all the Asian states, with the exception of India, Pakistan and Israel, have already signed the Non-Proliferation Treaty (NPT) as non-nuclear-weapon states, agreed and extended the NPT for an indefinite period into the future and are bound by the non-proliferation regimes and international agreements based on the extension and elaboration of the NPT principle. The non-proliferation order is being further strengthened. Thus a country can now acquire nuclear weapons only through clandestine means or by giving formal notice of withdrawal from the NPT. Either of these steps would entail severe costs and the incentives for such individual measures would have to be very strong. The probability of further nuclearization should be far lower than is generally argued, primarily in the West.

Iraq had a clandestine nuclear weapon program that does not appear to have been completely eliminated. In any case, there can never be complete certainty that it will not revive a weapons program at a later date, especially since its conventional military capability is bound to deteriorate in the future. The humiliation and privation suffered by the country, no doubt brought on it by its own leadership, is not likely to be forgotten for a long time to come. The country has displayed a resolve to bear a great deal of pain and punishment in pursuit of its policies and goals. The risk that Iraq will acquire nuclear weapons at a future date persists.

It is extremely unlikely that Israel will give up its nuclear weapons and ballistic missiles. In fact, there is little international pressure for it to do so. Even after the nuclearization of India and Pakistan, the Western world seems to have assiduously sought to leave Israel out of any calls for denuclearization or even for capping its capabilities. It is possible to argue that Israel may perceive its nuclear weapons as being even more important as a guarantor of its security in the long term, if and when a comprehensive peace is established in the region. With the expansion of its strategic and security concerns to the periphery beyond the Middle East, including Iran, Israel appears to be strengthening its rationale for retaining nuclear weapons in the future.

There is a widely held view that Iran is likely to acquire nuclear weapons sooner rather than later. If Iranian perceptions of its glorious Persian past and signs of future ambitions are any indication, it is difficult to believe that Iran will remain a non-nuclear-weapons state indefinitely. Sandwiched between two nuclear weapon states (Israel and Pakistan) with another antagonistic state (Iraq) that has pursued a clandestine nuclear weapon program next door, Iran's incentives for acquiring nuclear weapons capability appear strong. Its acquisition of ballistic missiles and an indigenous program to expand their capability would also support this perception. China, which has transferred nuclear weapons technology and ballistic missiles to Pakistan, is also a supplier of military technology and ballistic missiles to Iran. There are reports of Chinese cooperation with nuclear technology in Iran.[15] On the other hand, the International Atomic Energy Agency (IAEA) has been giving Iran a clean bill of health and there is little evidence to support substantive suspicions regarding Iran's quest for nuclear weapons. But if Iran does acquire nuclear weapons, other countries in the region are not likely to lag far behind, and the security environment in South Asia will become exceedingly complex. The United States may feel compelled to take counter-proliferation measures against Iran in order to preempt any such move. But this itself is likely to trigger many unpredictable consequences.

The only way to eliminate uncertainties about future nuclear proliferation is to make a decisive move towards the total abolition of nuclear weapons. India has pressed for such progress for many decades. It has proposed resolutions at the United Nations seeking a convention to ban the threat and use of nuclear weapons. The establishment of such a convention is essential in order to change the theories that have sought to legitimize nuclear weapons. Because of their rationale for their acquisition of nuclear weapons, Pakistan and Israel are unlikely to seek the abolition of nuclear weapons, regardless of the public posture they adopt. It is possible that India could become as cynical as the five acknowledged weapon states and start to pay only lip service to total nuclear disarmament. Some in India are starting to shy away from an unqualified commitment to the demand for the abolition of nuclear weapons. But India's interests would be better served by abolition.

Among the issues affecting Western Asia as a result of India's and Pakistan's acquisition of nuclear weapons is the large expatriate population in the region. There are more than three million Indians and nearly one million Pakistanis living and working in the GCC countries alone. There would no doubt be some concern as to what would happen if war broke out between India and Pakistan. This has happened before, and the expatriate population of both countries remained loyal to their responsibilities in the country of their temporary residence. Although the numbers have increased markedly over the years, there is little to suggest that the general tranquility that existed even when their parent countries were at war will change in the future. The increased human resource contributions of India and Pakistan to the GCC countries and their economies also implies the increased stake of India and Pakistan not only in the peace and prosperity of these countries, but also a necessity to insulate the expatriate population from the tensions between them. The GCC countries could also be a key factor in moderating the tensions in the subcontinent. But this would require them to maintain a neutral attitude to bilateral issues and problems.

3

Pakistan and Regional Security in South Asia

Najam Rafique

Although most security problems are often the product of global, regional and domestic developments, the major sources of tension in South Asia are legacies of the colonial past. In the final decades of British rule in India, some of the British functionaries in the subcontinent made intense efforts to promote communalism and hatred between Muslims and Hindus, in pursuit of their policy of divide and rule. This policy was consciously adopted by the British immediately after the 1857 Sepoy Mutiny, and formalized by organizing units and sub-units of the British Indian Army on the basis of religion or caste. The policy was designed to perpetuate British hold and had two main tenets:

- to divide the Muslims and Hindus into small princely states
- to promote fundamentalism so that the two communities that had lived in harmony for centuries, did not modernize and work for their mutual benefit.

The British were so successful in making the two communities antagonistic that the legacy carried on into the post-partition era of the subcontinent. It was later aggravated by the active involvement of outsiders in what academics refer to as neo-imperialism, during the Cold War.

In recent years, it has almost become a ritual to begin any discussion of security issues by referring to the end of the Cold War and the disintegration of the Soviet Union. And in most instances it is entirely appropriate to do so, for these two events brought fundamental and wide-ranging changes, both to the national and international security environment and to the agendas of nations. But in no region of the world do these events appear to have had less impact on the fundamentals of security, whether at the inter- and intra-state level, than in South Asia. Security problems in this region are mostly indigenous. All the countries of South Asia – Pakistan, Sri Lanka, Bangladesh and Nepal – share borders with India, and for all of them, the main threat emanates from India's policy of domination, its hegemonic tendencies and its sheer size.

Throughout history, very little has changed in South Asia in terms of security and conflict resolution. Several factors have contributed to the unstable security environment in the region and have raised more doubt and concern than hope and optimism, including:

- the Hindu-Muslim divide
- the dictates of "negative sustenance" emphasizing the dissimilarities between cultures
- the evolution of different sets of institutional arrangements ranging from parliamentary to military and monarchical
- a geographically-dominant India, which shares borders with all of her neighbors
- five major wars since 1947 between China, India, Pakistan and/ or Bangladesh, resulting in the dismemberment of Pakistan, the creation of Bangladesh and the absorption of states such as Sikkim
- demographic aggressions (Bangladesh-India)
- trade wars (India-Nepal)
- insurgencies (Kashmir, Punjab, Assam, Chittagong Hill Tract and Sri Lanka)
- high population growth, food insufficiency, poverty, illiteracy and deteriorating health standards
- the explosion of nuclear devices and the development of delivery systems.

Strategic Lessons

First, South Asia is seen by two generations as a region of strife, war and intractable conflict. The absence of cooperation between Pakistan and India has made the region vulnerable to outsiders and has made it hard for them to pursue common strategic objectives both within and beyond the region.

Second, well-intentioned offers of mediation or conflict resolution are seldom welcomed by India, and almost never accepted except under duress. In this regard, no issue has been more important and frustrating than that of Kashmir. Both Pakistan and India have refused to resolve, or at least suspend the conflict, in the absence of a compromise in the rival position. As a result, both sides have been diverting large amounts of scarce resources from urgent economic and developmental needs.

Third, because of the two countries' refusal to cooperate, the region has been torn apart and has been unable to build strategic unity in South Asia.

Because confidence-building measures involve such a heavy agenda, the states of South Asia find it convenient to pursue their strategic objectives in terms of access to external alliances.[1] The challenging task of state- and nation-building also makes it difficult for the regional states to set any standards for managing foreign policy. Demands for self-determination are not just confined to Kashmir, but exist in many other parts of India. The demand in Sri Lanka for a Tamil Eelam homeland has been a particularly bloody campaign. The security environment is further aggravated by religious and ethnic violence which has gripped the politics of India and Pakistan. In fact, threats to the security of the two states today stem more from internal upheaval and turmoil than from any external power.

At the heart of the security situation in South Asia lies the hostile relationship between Pakistan and India. "Partition's legacy has been a uniquely bitter brand of inter-state politics. Since 1947, Pakistan and India have been unable to agree on the terms of amicable coexistence."[2] As things stand today, it does not seem likely that they will be able to coexist peacefully in the foreseeable future. Neither country is willing to take the initiative and risks necessary to launch a genuine peace process at the cost of losing their parliamentary majorities.

Pakistan: A Brief Background

Since its inception in 1947, Pakistan has sought to develop its society rapidly and peacefully. Its infrastructure and development activities have yielded satisfactory results, and increased its manufacturing share in the industrial, mineral, construction and energy sectors. The country has moved from the first phase of industrialization, focusing on basic consumer industry, to the production of light engineering goods. Efforts toward social development, however, have not been as substantive. The majority of the population is still based in villages, with limited access to modern services, health and education. Despite promises to improve education, the literacy rate has not risen above 30 percent. Agriculture constitutes the mainstay of the national economy and over 70 percent of the country's population is engaged in agro-based activities. Agriculture employs 53 percent of the labor force, provides 30 percent of Gross Domestic Product (GDP) and 35 percent of foreign exchange earnings.

Pakistan's politics have oscillated between democratic and authoritative systems of governance. Following these experiments, Pakistan seems to have finally adopted a political system based on federal parliamentary democracy.

As a major country and a medium power in the region, the major focus of Pakistan's interaction with its neighbors in the region has been conditioned by challenges to its national security, territorial integrity and freedom. In this regard, it has interacted with other states, regional and international organizations and non-governmental organizations in order to protect and promote its national interest and mobilize support and resources for domestic socio-economic development.

The crux of Pakistan's security dilemma relates to its immediate geostrategic environment, which is often described as troublesome and hostile. While preservation of peace and stability at the regional level has always been the country's prime concern, the emergence of a multipolar world has presented new security dimensions. Pakistan and India's status as nuclear states also explains much of the heightened interest in the region. Relations with regional and extra-regional states have a major impact in determining the course of regional security in South Asia.

The Impact of Regional and International Actors on Pakistan

Pakistan–India

A pattern of relations based on conflict breeds a common denominator of deep mistrust between India and Pakistan. Although many people in the two countries think that any conventional war between them is unlikely, the chances of accidental or intentional nuclear war have increased following the May 1998 nuclear tests and the vigorous programs of missile development. The future of Kashmir which is the core issue, remains in limbo, particularly with the rise in Hindu fundamentalism as exemplified by the Bharatiya Janata Party's (BJP) ascendancy to power. India has been in unlawful occupation of Kashmir since 1948. With problems in Kashmir worsening, India has drawn the attention of the already frightened Western world to the threat that Islamic fundamentalism will emerge in the region. Real issues, such as those concerning the South Asian Association for Regional Cooperation (SAARC) and development, remain neglected.

Since 1950, successive Indian governments have been caught up in its insistence that Kashmir is an *Atoot Aung* (integral part) of India. This has presented an insurmountable obstacle to peace. Since 1990, the intense fighting in Kashmir has resulted in thousands of deaths and has cost both countries dearly, apart from affecting their international reputations. Although ten rounds of Secretary-level talks have been held between the two countries since 1972, new realities, whether international, regional or domestic, have done little if anything to spur judicious thinking on the part of the Indian government over the Kashmir issue.

The following points should be made about the Kashmir problem, which commands today's headlines, editorials and television coverage:

- Kashmir originally came into dispute because of British connivance after they divided India and withdrew. Pakistan has been living with the consequences for over fifty years.

- The leadership in India compounded the original problem when it turned Kashmir into a badge of its national identity and refused to accept the accession of the Muslim majority princely state, as in the case of Hyderabad and Junagadh.

- Subsequently, Kashmir came to play a role in the respective domestic politics of both countries.

- Kashmir acquired an unexpected military dimension after India crossed the international frontier at the request of its Hindu raja. Since then, the cease-fire line has become an extension of the international border. More recently, advances in mountaineering techniques have turned the most inaccessible part of Kashmir, the Siachen Glacier, into a battleground, although more soldiers are killed by bad weather than by bullets.

- Finally, there is a contemporary Kashmiri problem, which is characterized by a national self-determination movement among Kashmiris who look to Pakistan, Afghanistan, Iran and other countries in the Middle East as models.

While India refuses to even consider a plebiscite, as originally recommended by UN resolutions and accepted by Pakistan, various options to resolve the Kashmir issue have been debated. These range from joint control, a referendum and UN trusteeship to patience and independence. The latest solution under consideration in diplomatic circles is to divide Kashmir along the Line of Control (LoC) and convert it into an international border. But if post-partition history is to be the guide to formal discussions between the two countries, nothing short of a plebiscite would be acceptable to the people of Kashmir. Both India and Pakistan have fought three wars over the issue. With both now in possession of nuclear weapons and the means to deliver them, many Indian as well as international policy makers believe that Pakistan intends to use nuclear weapons, if threatened on Kashmir. With their experiences of bitter relations over the last 50 years, most Pakistanis now feel that the Kashmir issue should be resolved peacefully and not through war.

Pakistani Prime Minister Nawaz Sharif and Indian Prime Minister Atal Behari Vajpayee at their meeting in New York on September 23, 1998, had affirmed that they would solve bilateral disputes through talks and confidence-building measures on a number of issues, including:

- boosting of regional peace and security
- Jammu and Kashmir
- Siachen Glacier, scene of the highest battlefield in the world
- Wullar Barrage, constructed by the Indians at the head of the Jhelum river and in violation of the Indus Water Treaty
- Sir Creek
- expanding trade and commerce
- efforts to control the drug trade and terrorism
- working on visa restrictions and cultural exchanges.

As a result of this meeting, both leaders met again in Lahore in February 1999 with a renewed spirit of increased confidence between the two countries and established new channels of cooperation, including a recent bus service between the two countries. Prime Minister Vajpayee accompanied the first bus, which arrived in Lahore in February 1999.

Under the "operational mechanism" to build confidence, the Foreign Secretaries of Pakistan and India were scheduled to meet in Islamabad in March 1999, to follow-up on the tenth round of Secretary level talks held in September 1998. These talks which have been indefinitely postponed, aim at finding a mutually acceptable agenda, though the final decision will be taken only at the highest level. While the countries have agreed to refrain from hostile propaganda and provocative actions against each other, it remains to be seen whether these talks can move beyond the bureaucratic rhetoric of producing non-papers and idealistic official statements to achieving something constructive.

Pakistan–Afghanistan

No other country in the world wants peace in Afghanistan more urgently and acutely than Pakistan, which shares a 2000 km border with it. The traditional need for a buffer has disappeared. Instead of standing in Russia's path, Pakistan would now like to facilitate Russian access to the warm waters of the Arabian Sea over the road and rail network of the Central Asian republics and Afghanistan. Pakistan has been host to approximately 3.5 million Afghan refugees since 1979. There are currently 1.7 million refugees in the country. However, it is for the Afghans to decide the form of government they would like to have, though it cannot be denied that a peaceful and secure Afghanistan would be an asset to the whole region.

After the Soviet withdrawal from Afghanistan, the strategic value of the country, which had been so high for the West, and particularly for the US, diminished significantly. In short, the *Mujahideen* and their mission have lost all support in Washington and other Western capitals. Events in Afghanistan after the withdrawal of the Red Army have turned into a proxy war involving the interests of a large cast of outside actors, including Pakistan and Iran, which has hindered not only peace prospects but also the economic benefits expected after the emergence of independent Central Asian republics.

The military struggle in Afghanistan today has assumed the shape of a struggle between various ethnic groups represented by two major factions: the Taliban, composed of Pushtuns; and the Northern Alliance, represented by Tajiks, Uzbeks and Hazaras. In the most recent developments, the Taliban have for the third time since May 1997, gained control of the Northern Alliance stronghold in Mazar-i-Sharif and Taloqan, the capital of Takhar province bordering the Central Asian republics of Uzbekistan and Tajikistan; Taloqan is the hometown and a major supply base of former Tajik Afghan defense minister Ahmed Shah Masood, who fled to an unknown destination. This offensive led to the deployment of Iranian forces (270,000 men), and the conducting of military exercises on Iran's border with Afghanistan.

The Afghan war involved a culture of fanaticism, violence and the proliferation of small arms and drugs, long before the rise of the Taliban. Although the Taliban have gained control of nearly all of Afghanistan (90 percent), the legitimacy of its government has yet to be recognized by the world. In August 1998, the country had the taste of direct military reprisals which were inflicted on the country as an example of the "iron-hand" justice that can follow, if a situation becomes unacceptable to the West.

The regional players – Pakistan, Iran, Central Asian republics and Russia, having supported efforts for peace, are currently backing the two opposing sides in Afghanistan. Consequently the current strategic scenario is one of "negative involvement", which has blocked all attempts at finding a negotiated settlement. Efforts by the UN have become nearly ineffective since it became clear that no single faction – whether the Taliban or the Northern Alliance of Rabbani's faction – could control Afghanistan exclusively. The scenario promises unending warfare and is the single biggest obstacle to the new version of the "Great Game", that involves regional states and oil and gas multinationals seeking the bonanza that lies under Central Asian soil.

Pakistan–Central Asia

With the emergence of the six Central Asian republics there is relief among many strategic planners, who think that this provides not only strategic depth but further opportunities for expanding Pakistan's economic and strategic horizons. While the vision of a larger economic bloc comprising nearly three hundred million Muslims seems attractive, it must be kept in mind that these states are themselves in the process of nation-building and are economically unstable. Given the armed contest in Afghanistan, the proposals for construction of a US$30 billion gas pipeline, from Turkmenistan through Afghanistan to Pakistan and eventually India, have presently been shelved.

The Central Asian republics, particularly Kazakhstan, Turkmenistan and Uzbekistan are concerned about the events in Afghanistan, not because of Islamic activism but rather the effects of prolonged ethnic strife on their independence and domestic tranquility. The turmoil in Afghanistan not only blocks routes for oil and gas shipment to ports outside the Strait of Hormuz, but also threatens the precarious ethnic balance of power in the Central Asian republics.

From a security perspective, once the civil war in Afghanistan ends, Pakistan will be in a position to offer the Muslim republics of Central Asia the shortest land route to the sea. In such a case, Pakistan's own political and economic position would be immensely strengthened.

Pakistan–Iran

Relations with Iran, which have traditionally been friendly, are now becoming susceptible to sectarian (Shia-Sunni) forces. The presence of Iranian forces on the Afghan border casts a gloomy shadow over bilateral relations. Apart from customary diplomatic statements made by the Economic Cooperation Organization (ECO) and the Organization of the Islamic Conference (OIC) both seem to have taken a back seat in this regard. In all probability, Afghanistan remains a test case for Pakistan and Iran to determine whether they can work together on regional issues. The traditional pattern of governance over the last hundred years cannot be ignored by the two countries. Already, there are Iranian proposals to extend an Iranian oil pipeline through Pakistan and on to India, in order to not only improve economic conditions in the region but also to reach a huge market.

After the incident involving the death of nine of its diplomats in the Taliban offensive against Mazar-i-Sharif, Iran deployed 270,000 troops, including Iranian Revolutionary Guard Corps (IRGC), along its border with Afghanistan. Iran has accused Pakistan of supporting the Taliban. There has been pressure on the Iranian administration to use the military option against the Taliban. While the fact that support is given to various ethnic and sectarian groups by Iran and Pakistan is no secret, the scale of the Iranian military deployment has brought traditional friends to the brink of insanity. In their perception, the situation may pass to extra-regional players thus perpetuating poverty and dependence, although Pakistan has done its best to diffuse Iranian anger and anguish. While war obviously brings casualties and losses of all kinds, there is more depth to Iranian misgivings which are rooted in the successes of the Taliban and the reversals of the Northern Alliance. With Iran currently chairing the OIC, it remains to been seen whether it can be persuaded to reconcile with the Taliban.

Pakistan–Gulf and Middle East

Many Pakistani workers contribute to the development of Gulf countries. However, since the Iraqi invasion of Kuwait in 1990, there has been an exodus of these workers back to Pakistan. Now, in the post-war reconstruction phase, there are more competitors in the field. With many Pakistani immigrants not able to go back to work, the army of unemployed has increased appreciably, thus adding to socio-economic tensions at home.

Pakistan projects its Islamic identity in its foreign policy and pays special attention to promoting unity within, and forging ties with, the Arab world. This close Islamic association has left a strong ideological imprint on Pakistan's foreign policy. However, the OIC and ECO need to play a more effective role in cultivating mutually-rewarding economic relations as part of the economic cooperation and effort to promote South–South cooperation, with the goal of addressing their socio-economic problems. This will indirectly impinge on the security of South Asia.

Pakistan–United States

In spite of being a long-standing "trusted ally," events since 1989 have proved that the US–Pakistan Cold War ties have been severed, as new strategic and political realities emerge in the South Asian region. Among mounting fears of regional nuclear war, the US has chosen to issue specific sanctions and diplomatic pressure on Pakistan to curtail its nuclear and missile program. In spite of these pressures, relations with the US occupy a pivotal role in Pakistan's foreign policy. In the aftermath of the Cold War and the Afghan war, the United States and Pakistan have begun the process of building a new, mature relationship based on shared democratic values, common perceptions on human rights, joint business ventures and a redefinition of the strategic roles to be played by the two countries in South Asia, the Middle East and Central Asia. It has been made abundantly clear to the Americans that Pakistan's nuclear program has been and remains peaceful. However, Pakistan remains acutely conscious of the threat to its security and the need to settle the nuclear issue in the regional context and not according to the wishes of the United States.

Nevertheless, the US policy of building up India, its efforts to forge a strategic relationship with the country as a counterweight to China and its effects on military security in the region, remains of paramount concern to Pakistan. Two accords signed in New Delhi are illustrative: one signed by US Defense Secretary William Perry, providing for dual-purpose technology and joint military exercises; and the other, signed by former US Commerce Secretary Ronald Brown, supplying India with the economic assistance needed to play the designated role. However, by mending fences with Pakistan, Washington seeks to guarantee its quest for "double insurance" against a hegemonic India that may challenge American presence in Diego Garcia or the Indian Ocean, or block US access to the Pacific Rim markets. In such cases, the United States would need Pakistan as a credible ally. The United States also believes that Pakistan, as a moderate Muslim state, is capable of exercising a restraining influence on religious extremism in the region.

Pakistan–China

China and Pakistan have demonstrated a remarkable understanding of, and sympathetic attitude towards, each other's foreign policy goals. Both have on occasion adopted a mutually supportive approach towards the major regional and international issues, and have adhered strictly to a policy of non-interference in each other's internal affairs, mutual respect for each other's territorial integrity and sovereignty, equality and mutual benefit. China is currently preoccupied with its socio-economic development plan. The border talks with India have led China to play a prudent game of avoiding taking sides, and restricting its help through rhetorical support. Given the nature of relations between the two countries, improvement in China's relations with other regional countries is not likely to alter the present pattern of Sino-Pakistani ties.

Impact of Nuclearization in South Asia

South Asia became overtly nuclearized in May 1998. Following the nuclear tests by India and Pakistan, the area is being described as the most dangerous in the world. Pakistan and India have fought three wars in the last 50 years, and now, with both in possession of declared nuclear devices and the missile technology to deliver them, even conventional hostilities could easily escalate into nuclear confrontation. Even before the May tests, India and Pakistan were already known to be nuclear-capable states.

However, the much publicized argument that Pakistan would only use nuclear weapons as a last resort for its survival is not very convincing, since a small nuclear force, while a good deterrent, is always at a distinct disadvantage vis-à-vis a bigger neighbor. Any retaliatory response could cause major devastation to the smaller adversary. The failure of international forums to prevent India from pursuing aggressive policies towards Pakistan, and Pakistan's experience of depending on distant allies, makes it more of an imperative than a choice for Pakistan to maintain and develop a credible sovereign deterrence which will be the apex of Pakistan's development. However, it may be that a negative economic fallout produces a devastation deadlier than any nuclear exchange.

Apart from this consideration, the bomb is unusable by both India and Pakistan. In the event of any nuclear exchange between the two states, and depending upon the wind direction, the radioactive fallout will affect many cities in both countries, because of their geographical proximity. However, such considerations did not deter the US, when it made the decision to bomb distant Japan or declared its intention to use nuclear weapons to stop the Soviet Union and China from acquiring their own nuclear capabilities. In their current state of mutual hostility, it is improbable that either Pakistan or India can afford, or even wish to hurt unborn generations or render some areas dangerous and unproductive for decades.

The developments of May 1998 are also considered a threat to the existing non-proliferation regime, which had been developed so carefully over the last 25 years based on the Non-Proliferation Treaty (NPT) and Comprehensive Test Ban Treaty (CTBT). There is now strong pressure on the two countries not to proceed with nuclear weaponization and deployment and to sign the CTBT. Although the US Congress may give President Clinton waiver authority to get sanctions lifted, Pakistan is required to show "substantial progress" towards non-proliferation benchmarks which include:[3]

- the signature and ratification of the CTBT
- a restraint regime covering the nuclear weapons and their means of delivery
- an export control system
- a moratorium on the production of fissile material, pending negotiation of the Fissile Material Cut-off Treaty (FMCT)
- direct talks between Pakistan and India.

On the regional level, the nuclear explosions, instead of alarming anyone except the West, have only complicated matters. After an initial period of jubilation, both countries have discovered that they are susceptible to international pressure. The first victims have been the economies of the two countries, more so that of Pakistan, which has a foreign debt of US$31 billion and lower foreign exchange reserves. Although it appears that the US may not want to see the collapse of Pakistan's economy, the overall economic impact of testing nonetheless has been substantial. Also, it appears that nuclear testing, instead of bringing greater recognition regarding the nuclear capabilities and power of the two countries, has somehow circumscribed their nuclear options and served only to fortify the resolve of the P-5 and G8 countries to speed up their non-proliferation agenda for nuclear disarmament in South Asia.[4] Pakistan has made it abundantly clear that it is only willing to sign the CTBT and adhere to it, in an atmosphere free of coercion and sanctions, and if lending by international financial institutions is resumed. Pakistan will not however, give up its status.

In spite of international pressures to check horizontal proliferation, India's attitude remains of paramount concern to smaller neighbors such as Pakistan. This is the result of the Indian detonations of 1974 and 1998, its efforts to enhance its delivery capability by developing a missile program and the recent declaration that it possesses a chemical arsenal. Given the hostility and suspicion that have long marked Indo-Pakistani relations, such efforts by India not only fundamentally affect the security environment in the region and present Pakistani leaders with radical choices for preserving peace, but its mass destruction weapons and delivery systems also pose a danger to the countries of Eastern, Central and Western Asia as well. Although India has not conducted another nuclear test, it continues to develop and deploy aircraft and missiles that can deliver Weapons of Mass Destruction (WMD) to its neighbors and beyond. Such activities have contributed to an open-ended arms race in South Asia.

Indian Weapons of Mass Destruction

Nuclear Program

The Indian claims about the peaceful uses of nuclear energy today seem futile in the light of the Stockholm International Peace Research Institute (SIPRI) reports indicating that it has enough plutonium to manufacture 200 nuclear bombs or even smaller tactical nuclear weapons.[5]

India's nuclear program began in 1944 with the establishment of the Tata Institute of Fundamental Research (TIFR) in Bombay (now Mumbai), which forms the backbone of Indian nuclear research. By the 1960s, India had built up an extensive nuclear establishment, including three atomic research reactors named Apsara, Cirus and Zerlina. Fuel from the Cirus reactor which was built with Canadian assistance, was used for India's "peaceful nuclear explosion" in May 1974. During the 1980s, India built a number of unsafeguarded research reactors, all of which produce unsafeguarded plutonium. These have dramatically increased Indian production of weapons-grade plutonium. Currently, the total established capacity of these plants gives India enough fissile material to make as many as 40 nuclear bombs per year.[6] In addition to these reactors, India has built three more, known as Narora-1 and Narora-2;

and another at Kakrapar. In theory, each of the six reactors mentioned can produce enough plutonium to manufacture 12 weapons per year, and once fully operational, they would give India a sufficient stockpile of plutonium to build 72 weapons per year.[7]

Chemical/Biological Weapons

In August 1997, India admitted manufacturing chemical warfare weapons three months after its ratification of an international treaty banning them. New Delhi has made it clear to the world community that it is already in possession of chemical weaponry. This clarification came in the wake of a move to circumvent the signing of a treaty banning the possession or use of chemical weapons.[8] There are also reports that India has stocks of such weapons, which were left in the country by the Allies after World War II.

New Delhi's admission takes on an ominous dimension, when viewed against the backdrop of the sophisticated delivery systems that India has developed since its 1974 explosion. Considering the gas attack in March 1995 in Tokyo, it should be borne in mind that terrorist attacks may not be so constrained. India has an extensive chemical industry and its Defence Research and Development Establishment (DRDE), in Gwalior, conducts research on physical and medical protection against chemical weapons.[9] India probably possesses weapons using one of the highly effective nerve gases – Tabun or Sarin – that can paralyze chest muscles and suffocate the victim; these gases were originally developed during World War II. Indian chemical weapons are likely to employ binary technology, in which the weapon or bomb contains two safe chemicals that combine just before detonation, to produce a lethal gas.

Delivery Capability

India has an adequate delivery in the form of more than 200 attack aircraft including MIG-23/27s, Jaguars, Mirage-2000s and the newly acquired Russian Sukhoi-30s, which carried out attack exercises near the Pakistan border in Rajasthan, in March 1998. Apart from combat aircraft, India has developed and deployed ballistic missiles that are capable of launching nuclear warheads. Today, India possesses an array of missiles that enable it to project its newly acquired power well beyond its geographical boundaries. Of these, the Prithvi missile, with a range of 150-250 miles targets Pakistan specifically, whereas the intermediate-range Agni can deliver nuclear payloads up to a range of 1,500 miles. In all probability, the Agni missile will be the test vehicle for developing an Intercontinental Ballistic Missile (ICBM) called Surya. "Thirty-seven satellite control sites and ground stations monitor the rockets and missiles which can be fired from the various launching sites at Shriharikota National Testing Range at Baliapal and at Pokhran."[10]

Conclusion

Despite concerns about the slow pace of global nuclear disarmament, the disintegration of the Soviet Union and the improvement of relations with China, Pakistan is singled out as constituting the prime nuclear threat to India, whose anxiety has increased with Pakistan's success in reaching its objective of obtaining nuclear capabilities. India's nuclear posture, as it has evolved over the years, has the following main adjuncts:

- the use of nuclear energy for peaceful purposes
- the pursuit of general and complete disarmament
- the refusal to sign the NPT, enter nuclear-free zone arrangements or join bilateral or international agreements
- retaining of the right to test again if Pakistan were to take threatening steps to its covert nuclear capabilities.

The phrase "keeping its nuclear option open" summarizes India's present nuclear posture of strategic ambiguity. There is wide domestic support within India for this policy, because of two important considerations: first, the end of the Cold War and the disintegration of the Soviet Union has deprived India of its chief strategic ally, whose support was available *in extremis*, as during the East Bengal/Bangladesh crisis in 1971; and second, in spite of the US preference for India, US–Indian relations have not strengthened because the Clinton administration includes India in its list of countries that embody US concerns, including security and strategic issues regarding regional instability, human rights, non-proliferation of nuclear and space technology, Kashmir, free trade and globalization.

While professing peaceful use of nuclear energy, India's potential for and possession of weapons of mass destruction (WMD) does little for peace, since their deterrent value cannot be taken for granted. The Indian threat becomes all the more serious in the face of the BJP leadership's recent statements, including its president, L.K. Advani's declaration, "I think we have no option in this regard, Pakistan having become nuclear, China having been nuclear for many years now, India simply in order to have its dealings with these two neighbors on a level ground, must be nuclear."[11]

India has come a long way in the development of its nuclear infra-structure over the past five decades. It has already crossed the psychological barrier against the production of nuclear weapons by detonating the so-called "peaceful nuclear device" in May 1974. India has also been critical of the efforts on the part of nuclear weapons powers to maintain their monopoly in the nuclear field and prevent other states from developing this technology, even for peaceful purposes. In this regard, the Indians have been very assertive in advocating their legitimate right to develop and benefit from nuclear technology. As a result, the world has gradually become reconciled to a nuclear India and opposition to an Indian nuclear program has been waning. Despite the Indian refusal to sign the CTBT and the recent disclosure of its possession of chemical weapons, in direct contravention of the Chemical Weapons Convention, the absence of any international pressure in terms of sanctions or any reduction in cooperation with India in nuclear technology and delivery systems indicates recognition of India's nuclear status.

Such recognition calls for serious measures not only on the part of Pakistan but also of other regional states which have felt the impact of India's adventures, its hegemonic designs and the ambiguity of its actions. Maintaining a nuclear capability is therefore an imperative that Pakistan can hardly choose to ignore, in order to raise the stakes in any war with India and thus discourage it from starting any conflict that might lead to the use of nuclear weapons. However, nuclear deterrence does not render conventional forces obsolete. This, in turn, calls for a new look at the level of conventional forces that needs to be maintained for contingencies short of those that have to be dealt with by nuclear deterrence. So a conventional war between the two countries cannot be ruled out. As a result, integration of its nuclear capability with conventional force levels in a comprehensive strategy for defense has therefore become a vital security issue for Pakistan.

South Asia needs an approach that allows for parallel processing of many issues, disputes and wrangles – an approach that has the virtue of honesty. For a billion-and-a-half people held hostage by the hostility of the two major powers in the region, it is not hard to imagine what South Asia would be like if India and Pakistan were to co-operate, not only on bilateral trade, water and population, but on preserving the strategic unity of the region. Each would then, be truly counted among the great regional powers.

4

China and Regional Security in South Asia

Christian Koch

The nuclear detonations by India and Pakistan in May 1998 brought world attention to an area that is often overlooked in terms of its political, economic and strategic significance. Even within the broader region, events in eastern and Southeast Asia often appear proportionally more significant than do equally important developments in South Asia. The presence of two nuclear states has not only begun to change this international perception but has sparked serious discussion about the nascent balance of power equation in South Asia. This chapter focuses on the role that the People's Republic of China will play in the emerging regional security arrangement.

Some observations are justified at the outset. Despite the fact that the nuclear detonations by India and Pakistan in May 1998, catapulted South Asia onto the international political and strategic map, the unraveling of the bipolar Cold War system was a powerful force in re-shaping the regional political make-up. As a result of events in the late 1980s and early 1990s, new and powerful opportunities have presented themselves that have initiated the search for new organizing principles or a new world order. This search is a global, not merely a regional transition, although the effects on South Asia cannot be discounted. However, it is also an unfinished project, and the rules of strategic competition remain very much in process. The nuclear detonations by both India and Pakistan can be seen as a result of the changes taking place in the international political environment. While the decision to conduct the nuclear tests added a layer of instability to the overall regional balance, it did not change the strategic reality on the ground, nor did it cause a major new strategic alignment. In fact, many of the rules of the game that were followed up to May 1998 still apply today. What the nuclear blasts have instead done more directly is to focus intense attention on the strategic significance of South Asia (in addition, of course, to shattering a number of prevalent myths regarding nuclear non-proliferation and disarmament).

The emergence of a change in the structure of the international system has, in addition to focusing attention on the rising geopolitical importance of Asia, led to what can be termed an obsession with the threat from China, including an extensive concentration on China's military and economic power, all in an effort to project Chinese power potential into the next century.[1] There are, of course, numerous reasons for this fascination with China. For one, deservedly or not, China has always been regarded as a first-rate power, despite the fact that economically, and also militarily, it has lagged far behind the other great powers, such as the United States and the Soviet Union.[2] Second, China has vast territory, the largest single population of any nation on earth, vast resources, military might that includes nuclear capability and a relatively consolidated domestic political constituency. These factors combined make it essential to look more closely at the implications of a growing China. Third, China has never embraced the notion of transparency about itself, in particular with regard to its military and security activities, and thus a certain amount of mystique about the Chinese capability for projecting power has been added to the equation. Fourth, it has been recognized that the potential for a sudden political transformation, as witnessed by the quick collapse of the Soviet Union, cannot be completely discounted. So, while China seems to be politically stable at this point in time, a sudden shift toward greater domestic instability has become a lurking possibility. This instability, coupled with the obvious implications beyond China's borders, has underscored the necessity to pay close attention to the events surrounding Chinese development and growth.

China has been able to improve its international standing significantly over the past decade. Its concerted efforts to improve its national economy in the post-Mao era have paid substantial dividends. Indeed, China's Gross National Product (GNP) has doubled over the past five years (and tripled over the last two decades); its average growth rate has been maintained at around 10 percent for the past 15 years and many industrial as well as agricultural sectors have posted impressive gains.

China is now poised to become the world's second largest economy, after the United States, early in the next century.[3] On a social level, the staggering economic changes of the past 20 years have delivered, "perhaps the greatest reduction in poverty the world has ever seen."[4] These remarkable developments are accompanied by negative effects, including rising unemployment, a growing external debt and a looming banking crisis – just to name a few examples. Yet, even at this stage (early 1999), and despite being under intense pressure, China has managed to avoid the negative consequences of the Asian economic crisis, unlike its northern Russian neighbor. As a result, forecasts about the looming demise of China would be premature at best.

At the same time, since the late 1980s China has made a comprehensive effort to modernize its armed forces in order to be able to fight a limited war under high technology conditions. Based on the belief that military power is a central component of national strength and recognizing the fact that the country has lagged behind in terms of its military capabilities, the Chinese leadership has put a great deal of effort, both qualitatively and quantitatively, into enhancing its military power. In addition to double-digit increases in the defense budget, the availability of advanced armaments from an economically-strapped Russian military industry following the demise of the Soviet Union has provided a golden opportunity, in addition to removing one potential adversary, at least in the short term. China has also effected qualitative improvements in its naval forces, a step that will enable the People's Liberation Army to pursue Beijing's interests at ever-increasing distances from the mainland.[5] Finally, it has concentrated on the development of a comprehensive ballistic missile program, focused particularly on short-range, mobile and conventional improvements. These advances should be viewed as part of an effort to establish China as the dominant power in Asia. They are not aimed at trying to attain a global capability comparable to that of the United States.[6] Ultimately, China is determined to debunk the threat theory to show that it can provide a security system for Asia that will replace the US-dominated alliance system now in place.[7]

In the context of these recent economic and military developments and in order to put the debate about China's importance as a international power into perspective, it is important to measure its power in relative rather than absolute terms. Equally important is the distinction between perceived and estimated power – the former being based on certain historical contexts and current absolute projections, while the latter attempts to place China's growth both economically and militarily in the context of developments over time. So, while there is no doubt that China has made substantial economic gains over the past two decades, going from a small-scale international economic power to an eager, large-scale power that plays an effective role in the international economic arena, the low level from which the current economic and military growth began needs to be recognized. By the time China started its current reform process, the country was far behind other nations with a comparable international status. By conventional standards, China is a rising great power. Yet the numerous question marks that hang over its near-term future – such as whether economic growth over the past two decades can be sustained, whether increased military spending can be turned into a greater power projection capability and how far increased economic status can boost the formation of a strong Chinese national state or whether China will ultimately collapse due to its inherent contradictions – ensure that "China's future as a complete great power remains indeterminate, if not foreclosed."[8]

Notions of Asian Security

When looking at the existing and emerging regional security environment in South Asia, it is equally important to put the general discussion about Asian security into its proper context. First, it should be realized that no parity of forces has ever existed in Asia. Instead, Asia has always been a region in which there have been a number of states of almost equal power. As one observer puts it, "Asia's inter-state system has, from the outset, been based on a multipolar structure and characterized by open conflict and overt rivalry between its key elements."[9] Relations between states have not been stable throughout recent times, further complicating the multipolar structure and the uncertainties related to this system. Of all the inter-state conflicts that have occurred over the past few decades the majority have been in Asia, and the potential for further conflict is an ever-present reality. Today, Asia remains, "a vast continent of competing political ideologies and regimes, vulnerable minorities and volatile states."[10] This system of competition directly impacts on the current situation in South Asia and China's respective role in it.

Multipolarity, in fact, carries the possibility of greater instability as a result of the nuclear tests conducted by India and Pakistan. At its core, a multipolar system contains numerous antagonisms, which are reflected in different competing national interests that have to be accommodated. As a result, not only is uncertainty in the system compounded as a whole, in effect increasing the difficulty of policy-making, but the potential for an increase in the number of conflicts, although not necessarily their significance, is also substantially heightened. As Richard Rosencrance has aptly pointed out, "[A]tomic weapons superimposed on [such] antagonism[s] are a recipe for instability."[11] Already, Asia contains more nuclear powers or nuclear-capable states than any other region in the world. With no serious conflict resolution capability (discussed below) but extensive military modernization efforts, multipolarity in Asia, as compared to the bipolar structure of the Cold War, contains the seeds for greater instability, now that nuclear weapons have been added to the overall strategic debate.

Second, no overarching regional order responsible for managing Asian security exists, within which a single power reigns supreme. Recent efforts under the auspices of the Association of Southeast Asian Nations (ASEAN) framework or the Asian Regional Forum (ARF) have so far failed to change this situation – certainly these multilateral efforts remain mainly untested as far as a future security framework is concerned. As one observer points out, "[t]here was and is no common vision of the purposes of a security regime for the Asia-Pacific among the states of the region." The Asian states do not practice collective or cooperative security, rather there is, at most, a system in which an increasing number of mutual reassurances are provided about each others' peaceful intentions.[12] In fact, the argument can be put forth that these organizations have survived simply because they have managed to stay clear of tough regional and national security issues. This situation will not change until all members fully understand that constructing such a regime is a long drawn out process for which there are no available blueprints and the initiative for lasting integration has to come ultimately from the actors in the region themselves.

There is, therefore, a need to focus on the intangibles that make up the various power arrangements in the region. The consequences of the end of the Cold War system for Asia, the lasting threat perceptions that exist at the regional level as well as diverse issues such as growing ethnic tensions and economic decline all have an impact on the emerging balance of power in Asia. Looking at China's potential for growth in the context of the historical and present environment illuminates the type of challenging security scenario prevailing in Asia as a whole.

Chinese National Security Policy

Within these broader outlines, Chinese national security policy, whether from an international perspective or from a South Asian point of view, follows some clear premises and distinct patterns. At its core, China's security policy is concerned with the survival of the regime in power. In particular, the Chinese place considerable emphasis on preventing any repetition of the numerous disruptive incidents that occurred at the start of this decade. From a theoretical perspective, the Chinese practice *realpolitik* in the tradition of Carr, Morgenthau and Kissinger and are great believers in the balance of power approach to world politics.[13] The concern of the Chinese political elite about the legitimacy of the political system and its corresponding stability translates into a necessity to dominate its frontier regions, including Tibet, Xianjiang, Hong Kong and Taiwan, in order to prevent foreign influences from promoting discord and dissension.[14] Because of this, China's main foreign policy objective beyond its immediate borders has been to prevent the rise of a peer competitor in Asia, or at least to cancel out any advantages that a competitor might have by making alliances with other states.[15] On a broader and more abstract level, it also entails being recognized as the leader and spokesman of the so-called developing, "non-aligned" world. China takes great pride in portraying itself as a non-traditional major power that defends the interests of the "have-nots" in the international system.[16] This latter aspect plays a fundamental role in defining China's relationship with other states in the region, and in particular with India.

In specific terms, China wants to prevent the United States from playing the role of a regional hegemon in East Asia, to stop Japan from emerging as an equal rival for influence and power and to prevent an alliance being formed between the United States and Japan and possibly other powers, such as Russia, India or other ASEAN states, in order to counter the possibility of China's strategic encirclement. In terms of South Asia, China has applied this principle by trying to prevent

India from becoming the unchallenged dominant power by building a *de facto* alliance with Pakistan.

In order to understand the fundamentals of this approach, it is important to look at the way power is distributed and examine whether there has been a discernible shift recently in the distribution of power in the region.

China has not pressured its neighbors overtly in the past to accept its ideology. The country can be characterized as a revisionist state whose agents are employed in order to maintain the status quo. At the same time, China expects the same kind of restraint from its neighbors, in that, for example, it does not want to be pressured about its conception of human rights and domestic governance.

Even on a military level, China has practiced considerable restraint over the past decade. It can be argued that essentially, China represents what can be termed a "conservative power" in terms of its foreign and security policy.[17] While such a view is open to considerable debate, it can be argued persuasively that China is not an expansionist power in the traditional sense, and that recently it has actually deepened its commitment to becoming an integral part of the international community. The acceptance by Chinese leaders of their interdependence with regional economies, is a demonstration of this new mood of responsibility. So too, are the events surrounding the takeover of Hong Kong – a transition that has proven to be far less disruptive than originally anticipated. Responsibility is also reflected in the emphasis on multilateralism and peaceful coexistence in the Chinese Defense White Paper released in July 1998. The most compelling basis for such policy changes are to be found in the linkage between economic development and prosperity and military and political security. Chinese leaders are aware of how serious domestic problems could affect the country's stability and have thus emphasized economic security. With economic turmoil being classified as a national security threat, China's military tends to be cautious in its actions so as not to scare away essential foreign investment. However, this does not mean that the Chinese are ready to compromise on core national interests.

Counted among the major security threats to China are: Japan, Taiwan, the United States, Central Asia and Russia. Due to the location of these interests, China is considered primarily an East Asian power, while South Asia is only seen as secondary in strategic importance. China's strategic authority on mainland East Asia has been long established, a fact that explains why China does not accord South Asia a large degree of attention. As will be explained later, this is an irritant, seen from an Indian perspective. At the same time, there are indications that the Chinese emphasis on East Asia may be undergoing some degree of adjustment due to the nuclear explosions. I would argue, however, that China will continue to be primarily concerned with East Asian rather than South Asian affairs, at least in the short term.

First and foremost among its national security interests, China fears the renaissance of Japan as a world class military power. This fear has grown out of many historical legacies – a visceral distrust as a result of the atrocities committed by Japanese troops in the 1930s and the Chinese national perceptions that this has spawned. There is a strongly held belief among the Chinese people that Japan has never adequately repented for its past actions and this attitude that is central to Chinese perceptions of Japan today. As a result, Beijings's main objective is to prevent Japan from becoming a full-fledged power rival. The United States plays an important role in this equation, as China sees the United States as being a restraining factor in terms of a resurgent Japanese militarism. From this perspective, America's presence in East Asia is reassuring to the Chinese, not because it strengthens Japan's military forces but because it replaces them.

After Japan, Taiwan is the second major concern for China. Though not seen as a direct threat, the potential for future conflict over the issue of Taiwan has to be considered high. Taiwan is seen as part of the Chinese homeland and the Chinese are determined to use force against the island if it officially declares its independence. The 1895 defeat of China by Japan, in which Taiwan was ceded to its arch enemy, is still fresh in Chinese memory, and sovereignty status for Taiwan would be regarded as a threat to the national cohesion of China itself. This issue could take on an added dimension in the near future if one accepts the argument that communism as an ideology is slowly losing its grip on Chinese society and being replaced by a more assertive nationalism. While it would be unrealistic to expect a surprise military attack on Taiwan – as such a move would go against China's overall economic and political interests – Taiwan nevertheless represents a potential flashpoint that needs to be handled very delicately over the coming years.

The third consideration with respect to China's national security interests is its relationship with the United States which of course, is influenced to a large degree by the two aforementioned issues. During the Cold War, Beijing's ties with Washington were primarily influenced by the antipathy felt towards Moscow. Pakistan played an important intermediary role in improving ties between the two countries in the 1970s.[18] However, US–China relations ranged from being very friendly to being extremely adversarial. The key objective of Chinese policy is to prevent the US from becoming the sole hegemonic power in East Asia. China remains highly distrustful of American motives, and in particular its relationship with Japan and its policy towards Taiwan. The way in which these issues manifest themselves has a direct impact on the state of relations between Beijing and Washington.

The fourth consideration is that Central Asia has recently moved into the main sphere of Chinese national security concerns, for two main reasons. First, China is in desperate need of a secure and adequate supply of energy resources, having become a net importer of oil due to its economic expansion program. Statistics indicate that China's demand for oil and gas imports is staggering. According to one recent study, while China imported three million tons of oil in 1994, that figure had increased more than seven hundred percent to 22.6 million tons just two years later in 1996. The projections for the near future are even more astounding: 50 million tons in the year 2000 and over 200 million tons by 2020.[19]

In order to meet this demand, China has undertaken various measures to secure a relationship with the Central Asian republics, including the signing of border agreements with Kazkhstan, Kyrgystan and Tajikistan. In 1996, a confidence-building military agreement was signed by China with these states and with Russia during a summit meeting in Almaty. Further confidence-building measures, such as reduction in border forces, have also been implemented over the past two years.[20] The relationship with Kazkhstan is seen as the key link and the Chinese have even proposed paying for a pipeline that would bring Kazakh oil to the Gulf through Iran, from where it can be shipped to ports on the eastern Chinese coast, since the cost of laying proposed pipelines directly to China would be prohibitive. China's renewed interest in Central Asia should be seen in the light of establishing a long-term peaceful and stable environment, so as to be able to implement the economic development strategy that is central to the modernization of China.

The second objective in China's relationship with Central Asia is to limit the spread of religious fundamentalism and ethnic separatism into mainland China. This is an area in which India and China share mutual concerns and in which the policies of Pakistan and China have diverged. In 1997, violence broke out in the Chinese province of Xianjiang representing the worst incident of civil disturbance since 1949. The conflict between ethnic Uighurs in Xianjiang and Chinese authorities is being fueled by the situation in the adjoining trouble spots of Kashmir, Afghanistan and Tajikistan. As a result, China has taken steps to secure border areas intended to stop the infiltration of separatist elements and supplies to opposition figures inside China. Recent reports indicate that the Taliban, for example, is involved in training Muslim separatists for possible violent activities in the Xianjiang province.[21] China has responded by pouring billions of dollars into the region, resettling hundreds of thousands of ethnic Chinese in its western territory, as well as instituting various oppressive measures on its own population. The potential for increasing violence, however, and its subsequent effect on China's overall political stability, makes this an area of vital Chinese interests.

Fifth, China's security concerns also stem from developments in Russia. The country's preoccupation with its northern neighbor has undergone a significant transformation over the last decade: while the Soviet Union was once a strategic threat to China, Russia is currently a destabilizing factor due to the possibility of its implosion. As a result, ties have improved greatly between the respective capitals. With Russia no longer representing the strategic or ideological threat that the Soviet Union once did, China feels more secure about establishing extensive ties with the Russian federation. Serious progress has been made in terms of delineating the border between the two countries, and Russia has become a primary market for arms sales for the Chinese military. It might be argued that a weakened Russia has resulted in a resurgent China. At the same time, however, China looks warily at the possibilities of further disintegration within Russia. With its own economic problems mounting, China can ill afford the large-scale instability that might engulf large parts of Asia, as a result of Russian decline.

What is quite clear from the points discussed so far is that China's interests lie mainly outside the South Asian region. This has not been altered as a result of the recent decision by both India and Pakistan to undertake nuclear testing. Following the Indian nuclear tests, Chinese security planners concluded that these "did not constitute a grave or immediate risk to China's security."[22] In fact, issues such as the ongoing

Asian economic crisis remain of far greater importance. As a result, even in the short term China will continue to look to its east and west more than to its south. In a nutshell, China is more important for South Asia than South Asia is for China. Such a statement should not be misinterpreted to mean that China is indifferent to recent events, nor, in fact, that it has been indifferent over the past few decades. China simply does not view South Asia with the same degree of concern as it does other areas. Nevertheless, with nuclear weapons having been re-introduced into Asian strategic considerations, a closer Chinese look at the potential role of South Asia in its security planning is warranted.

China and India

Relations between India and China are critical both to Asian and global security. Given that the two countries together are home to more than one quarter of the world's population, their relationship is of utmost importance. In addition to the demography, the fact that these countries have a good resource base and that they represent emerging markets for goods, services and technology ensures them a central role in any future regional arrangement. From a Chinese perspective, India is the only country in Asia (aside from Russia) that has the size, might, numbers and intention to match China.[23] As one commentator has stated, Beijing perceives India to be an ambitious, over-confident, yet militarily powerful neighbor with whom it may eventually have to have a day of reckoning.[24]

The politics of the Sino-Indian relationship are not entirely understood, nor is the role of China in South Asia. To some degree, the exact nature of the strategic competition between China and India is puzzling. India's obsession with China is only matched by Pakistan's obsession with India. Yet, while there certainly exists a border dispute as well as a psychological rivalry, serious questions have to be raised as to whether this is enough justification to incinerate two billion people. Historically, relations between the two countries have been relatively good. Throughout the tenure of Jawaharlal Nehru, India saw China as an important potential contributor to regional peace, and Nehru himself envisioned the possibility of a Sino-Indian partnership in Asia. He stated in the 1950s that, "what mattered most to the peace of Asia and the world was how India and China behaved toward each other and the degree of cooperation they could show in their mutual relations."[25] Both Nehru and Chou en-Lai visited each other's capitals during this period.

During the same period, this relationship encountered difficulties with the coming to power of the Chinese Communists in 1949. China's increasing military assertiveness in Tibet, frequent border disputes (despite the generally favorable climate, there was never a serious attempt made to demarcate the entire border between the two countries) and finally the 1959 Tibetian uprising, the fleeing of the Dalai Lama to India and Chinese suspicions about Indian involvement in this matter, heightened tensions. In 1962, a border war broke out between the two countries, in which China was able to inflict a devastating defeat on the Indian forces.[26]

The scar on India's national psyche left by the 1962 defeat cannot be underestimated. There is a legacy of humiliation and grievance that remains a central component of Indian thinking about China. As a result, the notion has crystallized within India that the only language China understands and respects is one based on national strength. One of the most important lessons that India drew from the border conflict was that it would be extremely damaging for India to let down its guard. India assumes that while Pakistan represents the more immediate short-term threat, only China possesses the ability to threaten Indian vital interests.

Since the end of open hostilities, it has been Chinese policy to keep India in check by making alliances with India's neighbors. China has been pursuing a policy of indirect containment and encirclement with regard to India. It has also shown itself to be adept at the use of arms transfers as an instrument of foreign policy.[27] The central component of this policy has been the development of relations with Pakistan. But China has also placed emphasis on building ties with Sri Lanka, Nepal and Burma, all in an effort to isolate India. The growing importance of India's relations with the Soviet Union, culminating in the 1971 Treaty of Friendship, has been an additional impetus for China to look in the direction of containment. As far as India is concerned, this Chinese policy has cast doubts over long-term Chinese intentions. In order to avoid being intimidated during a possible future crisis, India has placed great emphasis on deterrence as a key aspect of its security policy.

In the run-up to the nuclear tests, Sino-Indian relations had once again undergone a period of improvement that some have termed actual rapprochement.[28] While the more conducive atmosphere did not lead to anything spectacular in terms of major breakthroughs, significant progress was made in trade and a dialogue on border disputes was initiated. There was also an impulse from each side to manage their relationship and prevent tensions from rising. Rajiv Gandhi visited Beijing in December 1988; China and India signed two peace and tranquility agreements, including one regarding troop and weapons reduction on the border; and in November 1996, Chinese president Jiang Zemin undertook his first visit to India in his capacity as head of state.[29] Even after the formation of a new Indian government under the more nationalist Bharatiya Janata Party (BJP), and just before the decision to go ahead with the nuclear explosions, China's Chief of the People's Liberation Army paid a visit to New Delhi in April, 1998.[30]

Nevertheless, the problems in the relationship have persisted. Large chunks of territory are still being contested; the Dalai Lama is still given sanctuary by India; China maintains its strong relationship with Pakistan and supports Pakistan's military establishment; and Beijing has continued to pursue a policy of military sales to India's other neighbors, such as Myanmar. India, meanwhile, continues to be irritated by the fact that China has never focused much attention on it, preferring instead to look towards Russia, Japan and the United States. During the Cold War, India played an important part in the power rivalry between the Soviet Union and China, although never between the United States and the Soviet Union. When the Soviet Union disintegrated in 1990, India lost a major ally as well as a source of political support. As a result, India found itself alone in its rivalry with China. Out of this situation has emerged the complaint that India is often ignored in Chinese policies. India also remains opposed to the freedom granted to China in terms of developing and modernizing its own nuclear weaponry, and sees China as wooing the US and standing in the way of India's aspirations. In this context, India argues that the difference between the two countries in terms of power and recognition is the atomic bomb (based on the premise that all great powers have nuclear weapons; India is a great power; therefore, India must have nuclear weapons), and that once the nuclear asymmetry is rectified, a border agreement between the two can be worked out. Still, this fact does not change China's strategy of hemming in Indian power and influence.

China and Pakistan

Given its size and capabilities, China possesses a capacity for mischief in India's vicinity. Nowhere is this more evident than with regard to the development and status of Chinese-Pakistani relations. For China, Pakistan represents a balancing factor in the regional strategic equation. Ever since the 1962 border war between India and China, the China–Pakistan axis has remained a cornerstone of Chinese policy in South Asia. Even when it has encountered periods of economic difficulty, China has always found enough resources to extend financial assistance to the leadership in Islamabad, although it should be noted that the relationship never evolved into a formal military alliance.

As part of the relationship, China has actively participated in setting up the Pakistani nuclear program, providing Islamabad with key technology, including the blueprint for an actual nuclear device. Today, Pakistan would have neither a missile, nor nuclear capability nor even enriched uranium, had it not been for Chinese assistance. The nature of Chinese assistance to Pakistan has included the tested design of a nuclear warhead, ballistic missile and missile components, fissile materials and nuclear plants, as well as ring magnets for enriching weapons-grade uranium.[31] Following the Pakistani nuclear tests, Prime Minister Nawaz Sharif specifically thanked China for its role and contribution.

From a broader perspective, the combined strategic and political advantages that China receives from its relationship with Pakistan easily outweigh any advantages that might accrue to Beijing from closer ties with New Delhi. From the Chinese decision-making point of view, if Beijing were to sacrifice its relationship with Pakistan in the hope of improving ties with India, it would ultimately lead to China's exclusion from the region on terms dictated by India. This in turn, would strengthen India's regional position at China's expense and allow India to focus its military resources on the Sino–Indian border. In that sense, Pakistan fulfills a key strategic objective of China's South Asian policy by preventing Indian hegemony over the region. At the same time, it is also important for China to reassure Pakistan of its support, so that the leadership in Islamabad does not feel the need to give in to Indian power.

China and the Rest of South Asia

China has also established relations with other countries in South Asia. As previously mentioned, following the 1962 border conflict, China began looking more intently towards Nepal, Sri Lanka and later Bangladesh, for ways to increase its ties in the region. Over the past few years, China has made extensive efforts to establish closer relations with Myanmar, in particular, regarding the use of port facilities for repair and maintenance for Chinese naval ships.[32] China has extended Myanmar about US$2 billion in military aid and established listening posts on the Coco islands in order to monitor Indian naval activity and missile testing.

Overall, China has become more independent and assertive in the 1990s, both in terms of regional and international politics. Part of the reasoning behind this transition is the fact that there have been some noticeable changes in the way China perceives itself. For one thing, China no longer sees itself as being solely a passive participant in the international economic arena. Rather, it has become an active player and is very much cognizant of the fact that on numerous fronts, it is urged to play a major economic role in the world. Militarily, China has moved from being a purely survivalist state to one that is beginning to actively shape the environment surrounding it. Basically, it pursues its interests by employing a two-pronged approach, first by strengthening itself on both the economic and military fronts and second, by active diplomacy. It should be remembered that what China wants essentially, is regional stability, in order to continue its economic growth.

Impact of the Nuclear Explosions on Chinese National Security Thinking

Did the nuclear tests actually change the regional balance of power from a Chinese perception? At the outset, it is clear that China was always quite aware that India would eventually declare its nuclear status officially. Therefore, the only thing that has changed as a result of the detonations is that India and Pakistan have now proven their nuclear designs. The rest of the equation was always known, and this being the case, there is no reason for China to now shift its regional strategy, since for the last 20 years, it has been based on the presumption that India possesses nuclear capability. Its long relationship with Pakistan is additional evidence that China was always aware of India's strength, particularly because the Chinese were heavily involved in the sale and supply of military items, including nuclear materials, to the Pakistanis. To date, China has not acknowledged that a strategic threat from India exists. In essence then, reaction by China to the Indian nuclear tests can be seen as a classic case of *realpolitik*. The Chinese are also quite aware that it will still take some time for India to establish an operational nuclear-strike capability.

The fact that China was singled out by India as the reason for its decision to detonate nuclear devices, focused attention on the future role that China would play in terms of regional security. Indian Defense Minister George Fernandes referred to China as the "number one potential threat" to Indian national security, and in addition to pointing out that Beijing supplied Pakistan with missile technology, he also accused China of stockpiling nuclear weapons in Tibet as a means of intimidating the country.[33] India has also claimed that an "atmosphere of distrust" exists in its relations with China and sees the unresolved border conflict as a background for the nuclear tests.[34] What has incensed China more than anything else, is the fact that India attempted to pass itself off as a nuclear counterweight to China while depicting China as a potential enemy.

Regional Near-Term Implications of the Nuclear Detonations

Under these circumstances, the focus needs to shift to the near-term implications of the nuclear detonations in relation to China. In this context, a number of possibilities can be identified.

A Missile and an Arms Race

The nuclear tests by India and Pakistan raise the stakes in what has become a three-cornered regional arms race. China is already a declared nuclear power, with a significant arsenal of weapons and various means to deliver them. Both India and Pakistan are thought to be capable of putting together nuclear weapons in a reasonably short time, although so far, neither claims to have deployed them. Still, China is unlikely to allow India to become a member of the nuclear club, since this would mean that China itself would lose its status as Asia's sole nuclear weapons state. The same ground for opposition applies in the case of Pakistan.

What is of greater concern at this stage is the danger of an accelerated, provocative missile testing phase. The nuclear arms race between India and Pakistan could very well spawn a parallel missile race, as each country seeks to develop medium- and long-range missiles that can ultimately carry a nuclear warhead, the only difference being that Pakistan's missiles are focused solely on India, while Indian missiles have to take China also into account. Weaponization itself is becoming an important issue. China and its arsenal are a prime factor driving India's weapons program. The fact that Pakistan's own missile and nuclear programs have benefitted from considerable Chinese assistance, has added to existing Indian concerns.

Whether a full-fledged arms race begins, depends on many other factors, including international pressure exerted on the states in the region, domestic politics, national economies and civil-military relations. Still, the expectation is that the short-term focus will be on nuclear issues, including the development of delivery systems, miniaturizing nuclear weapons and creating reliable command and control structures. The operative principle appears to be Mutually Assured Destruction (MAD) in its rudimentary form, with existential deterrence concept now part of the security calculations of both China and India.

There is no doubt that China has been modernizing its armed forces, as well as increasing its arsenal of nuclear and ballistic missiles. Due to this modernization program, the military gap between China and India has widened, a development that in all likelihood provided some of the rationale for the Indian decision to go ahead with its nuclear tests. Overall, however, there is considerable doubt about how far this modernization program will affect overall Chinese power projections. Defense spending has remained relatively low in terms of its share of GNP and the comparable spending of other large powers. Furthermore, the Chinese armed forces prior to any upgrading have been described as being in a deplorable state.[35] Any modernization effort, therefore, is unlikely to lead to noticeable change for at least another decade.

One particular area in which increased competition between India and China could become obvious, in addition to the ballistic missile arena, is in the naval field, where China has been determined to obtain blue-water capability, partly to counter some of India's advantages. With an 18,000 kilometer coastline and the lingering conflict over Taiwan, as well as Chinese claims to the whole of the South China Sea, adequate naval power projection capabilities are seen as essential, if Beijing is to maintain its regional level of influence.[36] But in this area too, China has a tough task ahead. For example, China does not yet possess a deployable aircraft carrier group and will probably not have one before the year 2010.

Despite Chinese efforts to improve its military, proliferation in Asia can only be prevented if China gets involved in the negotiations, and the Beijing leadership takes full advantage of this role. From an economic perspective, a classic arms race can be discounted, since it would be too expensive for the countries in the region to pursue, particularly with the continuing impact of the Asian financial crisis. The issue is not simply one of a diversion of resources, but of possessing these resources to begin with. Whatever the case, recent developments do point to the urgent need to put in place certain confidence-building measures. These could include a no-first-use pledge and effective command and control mechanisms in order to minimize the risks due to miscalculation. The key problem at the moment is that India does not believe in the pledge already given by China. Both remain suspicious of each other's long-term agendas and intentions. This should not, however, negate the need for an arms control process in South Asia. Equally important will be the nuclear strategic doctrine that will begin to emerge from within India. China will monitor closely its development and then decide whether an adjustment in its current policy of limited deterrence is required.

Shifting the Struggle to Central Asia

With the demise of the Soviet Union, Central Asia has become a focal point offering tremendous opportunities to the adjoining states, in particular as a source of desperately needed energy supplies. At the same time, Central Asia has sparked some concerns, for example, with regard to the issue of ethnic separatism spreading to adjoining areas. Such a scenario has already manifested itself in the increased unrest among the Uighurs of China's western province of Xianjiang. The region's economic potential, however, far outweighs the possible political and social consequences at this time. China has long regarded its western borderlands as holding significant commercial value and that continues to be true especially today.

The reason that this region could become an arena for increased competition between China and India, is particularly due to the fact that both countries look towards the region as an area that can satisfy their increasing energy consumption needs. The proximity of the region and the tremendous energy resources available there could very well spark increasing strategic competition between India and China when it comes to control over them. Lingering conflicts on its periphery, such as those in Kashmir and Afghanistan, could easily complicate the situation further.

Strengthening the China-Pakistan Axis

One result of the decision by India to undertake nuclear tests will almost certainly be to reinforce the existing alliance between China and Pakistan, despite the fact that the United States has begun to put considerable pressure on the Chinese to curb its transfer of technology to Pakistan.[37] While China has repeatedly pledged to end this cooperation over the last few years, a stance confirmed by US Secretary of State Madeline Albright, during the latest US-China summit in June 1998, raises doubts about Chinese commitment.[38] As has been argued elsewhere China remains a constant threat as regards weapons proliferation and has been identified as the most significant supplier of WMD-related goods and technology to foreign countries.[39] Pakistan's inauguration of a plutonium production reactor in March 1998 could not have been achieved without additional supplies of heavy water from China. Furthermore, China is said to have held talks with Pakistani military and diplomatic officials just before Pakistan made its decision to explode nuclear devices.[40] Pakistan's Army Chief, General Jahangir Karamat, visited Beijing in August 1998 as part of the continuation of high-level military exchanges.

From this perspective, it can be argued that the reports about military collaboration between China and Pakistan had reached such a stage in early 1998 that the Indian government felt the need for an adequate response. However, as China has little interest in allowing the nuclear arms race in South Asia to get out of hand, the supply of further nuclear equipment and expertise to Pakistan is likely to remain rather limited. Despite much of its recent activity, China worries about proliferation spreading to Iran, North Korea and ultimately, Japan. This is not to say that some degree of instability is not in China's interest. For one thing, an arms race diverts valuable resources away from India's long-term ability to challenge China for regional leadership. Second, instability in South Asia makes the region more unattractive in terms of foreign investment and development aid from international organizations as well as in terms of export markets in Southeast Asia – all of which are areas in which India and China are starting to compete increasingly. China will therefore attempt to maintain a fragile balance, in which it supports Pakistan to the point of agitating India but limits that assistance so as not to upset the regional balance of power significantly.

China as a Responsible Power

China responded to the Indian nuclear explosions with a mixture of caution and power diplomacy. While the verbal exchange between Beijing and New Delhi was heated at times, China in fact practiced a great amount of restraint, limiting itself to calls for India to act more responsibly and requests to New Delhi to mend ties. Beijing immediately signaled its willingness to join the United States in considering ways to reduce the potential for conflict in South Asia. In a statement following the nuclear tests, President Jiang Zemin announced that China would make every effort to curb the arms race in South Asia, to ease the situation in the region and to continue to push for the banning and destruction of nuclear arms.[41] Most importantly, no retaliatory threats were made against New Delhi. The result has been that China is seen as a more mature and responsible nuclear power than India, which is perceived as a rogue state.[42] What the nuclear detonations did was extend an opportunity for China to portray itself as being in the vanguard of efforts to stem nuclear proliferation – this despite the fact that Beijing's non-proliferation talk and its nuclear proliferation deeds contradict each other.

There is no doubt that playing such a role will add to China's positive image. Its immediate pronouncements were received well in all the major capitals of the world, particularly in Washington, as was the statement by President Zemin that China is not about to resume its own testing program – a fear that had been raised in the immediate aftermath of the May detonations.[43] This, in turn, has led to the possibility of greater political cooperation between the United States and China in the management of South Asian affairs, in effect also giving the Chinese greater access to sensitive American technology. President Clinton has already stated that resolving the nuclear issue in South Asia requires active cooperation with Chinese leadership.[44]

It can be argued therefore that if India had intended its nuclear tests to put China on notice, this strategy cut backfired. If anything, the nuclear tests have provided China with powerful opportunity to improve its international influence and reputation by accepting some of the responsibilities of a great power. During President Clinton's visit to China, in late June 1998, the countries issued a joint statement of concern over the tests, calling for the prevention of an arms race and strengthening international non-proliferation efforts, including the immediate and unconditional adherence by both India and Pakistan to the Comprehensive Test Ban Treaty (CTBT).[45] India responded to these calls by accusing both China and the United States of having a "hegemonic mentality."[46]

Whatever the Indian reaction, China is likely to emphasize its commitment to stability in the region – something that will play well within the United States and weaken the position of those inside American policy-making circles who claim that China represents a direct threat against the United States. China will also avoid any direct retaliatory threats against India. If China sticks to this line, the immediate impact of the nuclear tests will manifest itself in closer US–China ties, a development that is probably the opposite of what India intended. In addition, there is strong doubt that China actually wants to be the region's supreme force in South Asia. Until recently, China was seen as an international spoiler and regional troublemaker. Today however, it is being co-opted by the United States as a partner for peace and stability in Asia.

Future Prospects

There are indications that the relationship between China and South Asia might not be as competitive in the future as is feared. Traditional approaches to power do not provide a good guide for the future, as they have often underestimated how the presence of nuclear weapons can fundamentally alter thinking about the costs of war. Balance-of-power theory would suggest an increasing downward spiral in instability because China's growing capabilities will alarm its neighbors and in turn spark the creation of alternative alliances, as well as an extensive arms race.

Even under the aegis of a multipolar structure, balance-of-power stability remains far from secure, with each state's efforts to enhance its security posing a potential threat to which others will feel the necessity to respond. In this scenario, malignant natural perceptions feed worst-case planning and ultimately result in conflict.

On the other hand, both theories of interdependence as well as those of nuclear peace portend a more restrained Chinese policy in the region, since in each case, the costs of conflict become higher than the benefits. The bottom line is the proposition that while conflict is a necessary condition for war, it is far from sufficient to bring about war by itself. It should be assumed that the lessons of the nuclear revolution have been grasped by those involved. Thus, their effects should be seen as prevailing, in spite of the many other influences that might otherwise lead one state to wage war against another. While there may yet be limited crises between the nuclear states of South Asia that have survivable retaliatory forces, their outcome is more likely to be determined by the balance of political interests involved than by confrontation. Once a risk-laden military engagement becomes a serious possibility, there is a tendency to keep the conflict within bounds – as was evident during the Cold War. Therefore, one could expect the emergence of a regional Cold War with all the attendant dangers but largely manageable enough to avoid a worst case scenario. The cliché that, "there are no permanent friends and enemies, but only permanent interests" certainly holds true in this case.

For China, key domestic problems, the ability to carry out vital structural reform and the continued requirement for high economic growth will ultimately ensure that it seeks some degree of international accommodation. China's rise to greater power status will undoubtedly be unsettling and frequently difficult, but it is nevertheless important that it be able to manage the process itself. Any inability to do so will be reflected in certain negative consequences. Current developments inside China not only influence Chinese perceptions of the regional and international environment, they also extend to the perceptions of others with regard to China. In the event of any internal deterioration, there will be a great temptation for the Chinese authorities to focus attention on possible foreign interference, accusing regional states and the US of provocative actions against the Chinese state. This, in turn, would require responses from those accused and ultimately lead to an increasingly unstable strategic situation in the region. With mutual suspicion between China and India remaining high, and security in Southern Asia continuing to be defined primarily in political and military terms and not in economic terms, the lingering disputes could easily erupt into broader confrontations. The result could be a "Cold War" inside one of the adjoining states, such as Myanmar, a confrontation by proxy or a direct clash.

Equally important is the need to assess actual capabilities rather than presumed potential, since the latter could quickly turn into a self-fulfilling prophecy. Ultimately, the outcome will be determined by the nature and context of the current environment, by prior developments in the international system, by the relations among the great powers – in particular those between the United States, China and Japan – and by their respective interests, capacities and expectations of what lies ahead.

Due to the intrusive effects of globalization, it is increasingly difficult to predict the actions of populous states. China faces a difficult task, juggling economics with politics and strategic calculations while trying to balance domestic stability and regional interests. For now, the key to China's security will be predicated by the relationship that develops between itself, the United States, Russia and Japan, and the emerging balance that will allow each one to enjoy a certain level of influence in every part of Asia. As far as South Asia is concerned, China will continue to watch developments with a wary eye, but it will consider the region to be more of a nuisance than anything else.

5

The Future Strategic Balance in South Asia

Eric Arnett

India and Pakistan were founded 50 years ago in antitheses; India has sought to be an inclusive secular democracy, while Pakistan came into being because of the fear of some South Asian Muslims that they could not live safely under such a system – a feeling that led to the Two-State Theory and Partition. After five decades, India's national project appears to be succeeding, despite the challenges posed by corruption, delayed development and secessionist movements. Muslims have fared well in India, enjoying social mobility and political advantages that more than outweigh their occasional encounters with crimes of prejudice. Pakistan, on the other hand, seems to be failing as a state. It is militarily, economically and politically in decline, while other models of Islamic governance have eclipsed the founders' vision. From this perspective, Pakistan cannot hope to balance India's greater strategic power. Although nuclear weapons are sometimes invoked as a means of balancing this asymmetry or deterring any predilection India may have to use them, a more accurate appraisal would characterize nuclear weapons primarily as a distraction for the Pakistani electorate and other key constituencies.

India as a Secular Democracy
Although India ultimately accepted the Two-State Theory and Partition, its founders did not see the need for a separate Muslim state and tried to prove that one was unnecessary by offering legal and social protection to minorities, including Muslims. Indeed, millions of Muslims remained in India after partition, and according to some estimates, the Muslim population of India exceeds that of Pakistan. India's electoral system

has continued to allow a balanced representation of a wide range of constituencies, even as intolerant Hindu movements have arisen. Political power has been transferred peacefully after elections, and civil-military relations have generally been healthy, if eccentric at times. Since economic reform and liberalization began in the early 1990s, the economy has grown at a rate previously thought unachievable, given socio-political constraints, and India's economy is now among the 10 or 20 largest in the world.

Despite this generally positive picture, challenges remain to India's continued development as an inclusive, secular democracy. Although intolerant Hindu movements have been contained and balanced politically, they continue to grow. They feed and are fed by secessionist movements, most notably the one in Kashmir. Furthermore, the weakening of India's national government, as a result of regionalism, concerns over corruption, the decline of the Congress Party and its enthusiasm for centralism, are bringing the efficacy, if not the viability, of democracy into question. It remains to be seen whether the shedding of Nehruvian economics will lead to sustained growth, given the deep-seated ambivalence toward consumerism, markets and foreign investment.

Nevertheless, the outlook for India's national project is more positive than negative. Governments are likely to remain weak and corruption will be a problem; rapid growth rates and development will not necessarily last. But more importantly, minorities will continue to prosper, even if they will not be allowed to secede. Within a few years, the permanent frontiers of the state are likely to be firmly established. Even without a border agreement with Pakistan, there is little prospect that the status of Kashmir will change meaningfully.

Pakistan as an Islamic State

With India having accepted the Two-State Theory and no longer seriously considering the reintegration of Pakistan (if it ever did), the latter's fate as an independent Islamic state is secure. Islam remains the shared belief system of the elite and the masses, even if there are differences of opinion about its interpretation. The Muslim League, created by Mohammad Ali Jinnah, the founder of the Two-State Theory and the state, remains the dominant political force. The brief challenge it faced from the Pakistan People's Party is seemingly spent. Democratic institutions were strengthened in 1997, when the president's power to dismiss the government was abolished.

Nevertheless, the crisis that led to the creation of Bangladesh in 1971 suggests a flaw in the Two-State Theory: Islam alone is insufficient to create an integrated state out of varied cultures. After decades of accommodation and repression, regional and Mohajir (and now Afghan) populations remain disaffected in the remaining areas of Pakistan. The perception that the government of Prime Minister Mohammad Nawaz Sharif is using his unprecedented political power mainly to enrich the Punjab at the expense of Sindh was significantly strengthened during 1998.

Violence between Muslims in Pakistan, as well as Pakistan's role in Afghanistan, has reinforced the negative – and often over-simplified – perceptions of critics that Muslims do not seem to make good neighbors but are more likely to be in conflict with other Muslims than with real or perceived enemies from outside the *Ummah*. Unfortunately, the military has played a part in fomenting intolerance, both during its intervention in politics during the Zia years and in its training of the *Mujahideen* to fight in Afghanistan and Kashmir. Now, as during the military dictatorship, Islam and the *Shariah* are used as political weapons rather than the inspiration for good government. Simplistic or self-serving interpretations also appear to have inhibited a dispassionate analysis of the nation's ills.[1]

The 1990s have seen a decline in Pakistan's economy and its military power, accompanied by deepening mistrust of the government. However, while religious differences and incomplete integration are likely to remain problems, a further division of the state appears unlikely, as does any hope of the integration of Kashmir into the nation, whether by political or military means. The burden of military expenditure on the economy is readily acknowledged by politicians across the ideological spectrum and indeed, by the military leadership. But with the emergence of a belligerent government in India after the March 1998 elections, the national project is now seen more in terms of security than of economics. Even under the difficult conditions created by Pakistan's struggle against decline, society remains vibrant. It is not yet clear whether further political development will allow that vibrancy to overcome the current malaise and enjoy fuller democratic expression.

Nuclear Weapons and Strategic Balance

Despite the hope of the Pakistani leadership, the nuclear factor has not altered the fundamental reality of their country's inferiority and continuing relative decline. While nuclear weapons may offer psychological reassurance to the Pakistani elite and a polity on the verge of despair, they appear to have had little effect on the military balance in the region. India still plans to fight and win a long conventional war, with its nuclear capability deterring Pakistani first-use of nuclear weapons. Despite statements and activities meant to bolster the credibility of Pakistan's deterrent, it is unlikely that the Pakistani leadership would authorize first-use in a war that has limited aims, such as a punitive attack relating to escalation of the Kashmir insurgency. Even if Pakistan did use nuclear weapons first, it is likely that India could continue to fight and win, even without responding in kind.[2]

Pakistan's Deterrent to Conventional War

After the 1971 war demonstrated that Pakistan could not depend on China or the United States to provide meaningful security guarantees, the government decided that it needed to develop nuclear weapons to offset India's conventional superiority. By 1980, the feeling that nuclear capabilities would create opportunities in Kashmir was taking hold in Pakistani military circles,[3] the theory being that nuclear weapons would deter a major conventional response from India if Pakistan crossed the Line of Control (LoC) or turned up the heat on the insurgency. Thus Pakistani nuclear capabilities were meant to deter conventional war even before any nuclear weapons had been created.

In 1987, the first major military crisis since the 1971 war reinforced the Pakistani perception that the nuclear factor makes war impossible. The perception had become so pervasive by 1990 that the president and foreign minister reportedly made strong statements that nuclear weapons would be used in order to maximize the deterrent effect of Pakistan's capabilities. Ghulam Ishaq Khan, the president at the time and the political leader who has taken the greatest interest in Pakistan's nuclear planning, told a journalist, "In the event of war with India, Pakistan would use nuclear weapons at an early stage."[4] Foreign Minister Sahibzada Yakub Khan is reported to have made his threat directly to his Indian counterpart, the future Prime Minister I. K. Gujral.[5] In fact, the capability to deliver nuclear weapons from aircraft reportedly was not created until after 1990 crisis.[6]

Since then, officials have made very direct statements about Pakistan's intention to use nuclear deterrence to prevent conventional war, and nuclear weapons now figure prominently in the national consciousness. The ability of nuclear weapons to deter conventional war was specifically cited by Prime Minister Nawaz when he sought to explain his decision to authorize Pakistan's tests, "These weapons are to deter aggression, whether nuclear or conventional."[7] A similar view was put forward more explicitly by Lieutenant General Asad Durrani, the former director of Inter-Services Intelligence (ISI) and former director of the National Defense College:[8]

> Our deterrence is already working . . . Our aim is to prevent war, also a conventional one . . . The effectiveness of our deterrent lies in a known or a perceived capability, and in the notion that we might have a desperate propensity to use it.

Despite the deepening faith that Pakistani officials apparently have in nuclear deterrence, the Indian military still plans to retain a conventional-war option, using its nuclear capabilities to deter first-nuclear-use. The Kashmir insurgency cannot succeed unless an unacceptable toll is inflicted, but India appears ready to wage conventional war rather than capitulate if the situation deteriorates to that point. Pakistan's emphasis on deterring war or using nuclear weapons early in a war could lead planners to neglect preparations for a long conventional war, an oversight that could compound the possibility of defeat and runs greater risk of nuclear instability.

Furthermore, Pakistan's reliance on an ambitious concept of deterrence requires regular threats and the flouting of global norms, both of which undermine the country's international standing and its foreign policy – with India and with more impartial interlocutors. No state in the international system, other than Pakistan, seeks so regularly to draw attention to its nuclear capabilities and its intention to use them early in war. China and India both have declared that they will only use their nuclear weapons in retaliation after being subjected to a nuclear attack, and never against any non-nuclear weapon state. France, Russia, the United Kingdom and the United States have all made it clear that they consider nuclear weapons as weapons of last resort. Nuclear threats are few and far between, even if there is a possibility of first use.

Under the circumstances, Pakistan is likely to weaponize its nuclear capability in the hope of increasing its deterrent effort. Given the domestic popularity of Pakistani support for the Kashmir insurgency in the wake of the Kargil crisis and the depth of the culture of deterrence among Pakistani elites, creating a credible nuclear deterrent is likely to be a high priority for the political leadership and the army. In order to make nuclear first-use a plausible option, Pakistan is likely to develop tactical missiles.[9] These in turn, would require the production of special nuclear material and several missile tests.

Even with this considerable investment of resources and political capital, the Pakistani promise to use nuclear weapons may not be made good in a crisis. As long as India's objectives are only limited, there will always be an incentive for Pakistan's leadership to postpone nuclear first-use. What India's military planners and concerned observers can never be sure of is whether the incentive not to launch first is strong enough to overcome the cultural conditioning that has been ingrained in the deterrence mentality of the Pakistani armed forces and political elite.[10]

India's Deterrent to Nuclear First–Use

India's nuclear weapon program, like that of Pakistan, can be traced directly to the 1971 war. Although India had already established a nuclear power project, its application to a weapons option was not developed until the confrontation between the United States and India during that war, which included a particularly acrimonious meeting between Indian Prime Minister Indira Gandhi and US President Richard Nixon.

Less than three years later, Indira Gandhi's political problems created an incentive for India to demonstrate its ability to make a nuclear bomb. Strictly speaking, a test was not necessary for the development of a weapon and would not necessarily lead immediately to its development and deployment.[11] But the test of a nuclear explosive device in 1974 demonstrated that India was prepared to defy the order that the superpowers were attempting to impose.

As early as 1979, while their Pakistani counterparts were developing and promoting the theory that nuclear deterrence would create freedom of action in Kashmir, Indian military planners were already considering the option of a conventional counterforce against Pakistani nuclear delivery systems. Following the typical Cold War logic of damage limitation,

Major-General D. K. Palit suggested that India would respond to a future Pakistani attack, despite the presence of nuclear weapons, with a combination of conventional counterforce and air defense:[12]

> India's defensive strategy against a likely nuclear conventional attack by Pakistan must aim, first of all to minimize the actual nuclear threat. In this case Pakistan's weak point will be its delivery system, because for a considerable time to come, its only recourse will be the fighter-bomber, of which the Mirage is the most suitable.

Before the 1998 tests, Indian officials had spoken and written about their doubts that Pakistan had mastered the technology of uranium enrichment, as claimed by Pakistani officials. The former head of the Atomic Energy Commission P. K. Iyengar in 1994 said that he doubted "there is any proof that Pakistan has this capability" to make nuclear weapons.[13] Raja Ramanna, his predecessor and the "father of the Indian bomb" (if anyone deserves that epithet) elaborated:

> From our experience in using centrifuges to enrich uranium, we know that these are difficult to maintain. And given the state of their industrial capability, it is apparent that Pakistan's plant is working nowhere to the capacity planned . . . In the past, Pakistan got plenty of mileage by making tall claims. But that is now turning into paper mileage.[14]

This scientific skepticism may have been a factor in Indian military planning. Before the 1998 tests, the Indian military may not have "believed that Pakistan had a viable deterrent," according to P. R. Chari, former Additional Secretary of Defense, the second ranked civilian responsible for the Indian Air Force.[15] Former Chief of Army Staff General V. N. Sharma shared this view "I don't see any threat of nuclear capacity or capability in Pakistan."[16] Even after the tests, Indian military planners are likely to maintain their confidence that a conventional war can be fought below the nuclear threshold. From their perspective, Pakistan would not dare to use nuclear weapons first because India has the means to retaliate "in the range of ten megatons for one," in the words of a retired Indian chief of army staff.[17]

Although India's nuclear policy is more restrained than Pakistan's, it is not without its problems. Most obviously, India cannot be confident that a conventional attack would not lead to Pakistani first-use, even with an ambitious effort to maintain nuclear survivability, if not superiority. Furthermore, the short-term trend on the Indian side is toward deferred or "recessed" deployment, which entails a slower response to crises. Moreover, the continued civilian custody of nuclear weapons that has characterized Indian nuclear policy undermines the development and rehearsal of procedures, and therefore inhibits safety and stability.

Over the longer term, India's nuclear posture may not remain as restrained as it has been. At present, the greatest challenge to the policy of deferred deployment is the political ascendance of the Defence Research and Development Organisation (DRDO), which could distort policy. The DRDO, which has enjoyed a 70-percent increase in its budget over the last two years,[18] has developed two ballistic missiles – the Prithvi short-range missile and the Agni intermediate-range missile – for which the armed forces have no formal requirement. For its part, the DRDO is attempting to refute the claim that it does not deserve such a large part of the defense budget by bringing some of the major systems it has developed into service. Although there is no need for India to deploy the Agni – and especially not an extended-range Agni 2 – unless the relationship with China deteriorates,[19] Indian domestic politics could push the system through to deployment, possibly aggravating the Chinese perception of the current government in Delhi. In this scenario, the Agni 2 would be developed and produced through a combination of DRDO's political clout and the desire of leading politicians to demonstrate their willingness to do something that the US Government has specifically said it opposes. Producing and deploying the Agni 2 would require a strategic rationale, however, and that would no doubt be articulated as a necessity to deter China, even in the absence of any change for the worse in their relationship, which has steadily improved over the last ten years.

It must be noted that while Indian officials sometimes claim that their nuclear policy is driven in part by the fear of China, India has not purchased delivery systems capable of attacking Chinese targets beyond the Tibet plateau. Although this may soon change with the delivery of long-range, refuelable Su-30 aircraft configured for strike, and the development of a longer range Agni 2 ballistic missile, the record until now remains clear.

For the time being, India's nuclear force is likely to be limited and its deployment deferred. No ballistic missiles or additional special nuclear material are needed at present. Unlike Pakistan, India's nuclear posture does not require regular, overt threats or demonstrations of hostile or reckless attitudes. Nor does it challenge the norms of behavior with respect to nuclear forces and threats established by the nuclear weapon states party to the nuclear Non-Proliferation Treaty (NPT).

Air Power: Strategically Decisive

Contrary to common belief, the key to India's strategic superiority is its conventional armed forces, especially its air force.[20] The Indian Air Force (IAF) has achieved air superiority in all of the wars with Pakistan, and its advantages have increased with the introduction of new technology in the 1990s, a decade during which Pakistan has had to rely almost exclusively on China, the least advanced of the major arms suppliers. As a result, Pakistan has had to develop strategies that fall short of war in order to pursue its conflicts with India, especially over Kashmir. Indeed, its nuclear capability is intended to ensure that war will not break out, so that Pakistan can pursue its aims by other means. Nevertheless, Indian planners still apparently believe that war is an instrument of politics by other means and that nuclear weapons preserve the option of force and so deter escalation in the Kashmir insurgency. As V. P. Malik, the Army Chief of Staff stated after the tests, Indian nuclear weapons are perceived as a deterrent to Pakistan's "fueling more insurgency in its territory."[21] Before Pakistan can inflict sufficient pain for India to change its position on Kashmir, India is likely to exercise the option of conventional war. In that case, the choice facing Pakistan would be between accepting defeat or enduring an even greater catastrophe.

India's Recent Gains
India has gained air superiority in all three previous wars with Pakistan and its advantages in the air are increasing. The gap has widened substantially since 1990, when the last major crisis over Kashmir erupted, after which both sides apparently weaponized their nuclear capability. In addition to

taking delivery of a number of high-profile major weapon systems, India either ordered or took delivery of inexpensive but militarily significant components and command and control technologies, notably laser-guided systems (delivered) and an Airborne Warning and Control (AWAC) aircraft (reportedly on order).[22] Indeed, until the May 1998 nuclear tests, India was receiving advanced military technology from every major supplier except China, while Pakistan was cut off from such sources of supply.[23]

India's advantages not only include the benefits of air superiority, but offer the opportunity to neutralize Pakistan's nuclear deterrent. Offensive counter-air measures are the priority of the Indian Air Force (IAF) and its main area of improvement in the 1990s. While Pakistan's nuclear warheads may be stored elsewhere, all of its nuclear delivery systems are believed to be stored at air bases.[24]

While these capabilities give India the edge in a conventional war, and no doubt contribute to the military's confidence, there are weaknesses. Half of the IAF's Soviet-supplied aircraft are not operational, while the indigenous Light Combat Aircraft (LCA) has been set back by the cut-off in US technology imposed after the nuclear tests. The IAF still has very little by way of strategic defense. Even if these weaknesses can be redressed, the offensive counter-air campaign in which the IAF has invested so much may never be authorized due to the risk of nuclear escalation.

The key to India's maintenance of its strategic air capability will be the decision on whether to make or buy its next generation of aircraft. Despite the major disruption suffered by the indigenous LCA program in 1998, it is still the policy of the Indian government to phase out the MiG-21 over the next 10 years in favor of the LCA, which would then be augmented with an indigenous strike capability. Even if this path is not taken – that is, even if the IAF is not saddled with an inferior aircraft for the sake of national pride – the resources committed to indigenous military research and development are likely to cut into the procurement budget. If the funds allocated to the DRDO continue to rise, within a defense budget that is constrained, it will prove difficult to afford imported platforms in significant numbers, even if the costs of nuclear weaponization are foregone or strictly limited.

Pakistan's Desperation

Sub-optimal procurement decisions could make Pakistan's problems worse, too. In Pakistan, the Army, not the Pakistan Air Force (PAF), dominates procurement decision-making. Although the PAF's base complex has expanded since 1971 and enjoyed improvements achieved with the help of US advisors in the 1980s, the armed forces and the national leadership may not take the issue of survivability seriously enough. While PAF planners are certainly aware of their weaknesses, the decision-makers in the armed forces and the political leadership seem to discount the problems, because nuclear deterrence or the option of early first use make survivability seem an academic matter.

While these problems certainly existed before, they have been aggravated since 1990, when Pakistan was virtually cast adrift by the major arms suppliers. By 1998, the Pakistani military had grown very sensitive to the decline in its conventional military capabilities. Between 1990 and 1995, the country became dependent on Chinese arms that are far from the state-of-the-art. Pakistan's loss of its arms suppliers to India led not only to a loss of capability, but also to a feeling of abandonment and resentment. As Asghar Khan, a retired Air Marshal, said in March 1998, "We have neither support from our friends, nor have any military equipment, or new aircraft."[25] Mohammad Sarwar Cheema, chairman of the National Assembly's Standing Committee for Defense Affairs, agreed, "The order in conventional arms . . . has now been disturbed to a great extent."[26]

That feeling of abandonment has reinvigorated the military's interest in nuclear deterrence against conventional war. Pakistani officials have been making statements intended to signal that their nuclear capability should make India reluctant to use conventional force. Former ISI Director Durrani specifically links Pakistan's interest in using nuclear weapons first, in the early stages of a hypothetical war, to Pakistan's conventional inferiority:

> Because of its known deficiencies in conventional forces, [Pakistan is] likely to pull the nuclear trigger . . . In view of the upgraded potential that India should now be assumed to possess, we must be prepared to unleash our potential before it could be seriously impaired.[27]

There is no immediate way out of this impasse. For the time being, Pakistan can only address the survivability problem with mobile missiles, including plans and procedures for flushing them from their garrisons in times of crisis while maintaining communications and control. Beyond that, even a massive increase in procurement will not redress the disparity, despite the statements of Pakistani diplomats, who have advocated conventional arms sales as a stabilizing measure.

Conclusion

Implicit in this description of a militarily confident and ascendant India facing a declining Pakistan that sometimes appears to verge on desperation are a number of conclusions that merit more explicit exposition. These bear on the continuing risk of war and on the role of external actors concerned about the potential for disaster.

Implications for the Risk of War

Most significantly, the preceding discussion makes clear that war is still possible between India and Pakistan, despite the hopes of Pakistani deterrence theorists and their academic apologists. Furthermore, in the event of war, escalation to nuclear first use is possible. Significantly, war and nuclear escalation are as likely to stem from different beliefs about the likelihood of war and escalation, embedded in military doctrines on both sides, as by accident or unauthorized use. Nuclear war could happen by rational design as easily as by mistake, if not more easily.

That said, arms control has a relatively small role to play in managing the risks. The greatest danger arises from continuing conflicts and perceived opportunities to exploit the adversary's military inferiority or risk aversion, rather than from structural instabilities inherent in nuclear weapon systems. Even if the reverse were the case, there does not appear to be much room for developing a shared framework for evaluating the stabilizing or destabilizing nature of certain nuclear systems. Indeed, some systems generally viewed as destabilizing in other contexts – for instance, Pakistani mobile ballistic missiles – offer important benefits for survivability in the South Asian context. In any case, the treaties that India and Pakistan are being asked to sign – the test ban and a fissile material treaty – are not likely to have much affect on the risks involved.

Far more important will be a realistic understanding, both of Kashmir and of Indian ascendancy, on the part of the Pakistanis. While it probably cannot be articulated publicly, an acceptance that Kashmir's status is unlikely to change meaningfully must inform Pakistani foreign policy and its attitude toward détente with India.

Implications for Concerned Parties

Although the ability of arms control to address the problem of nuclear stability and strategic balance in South Asia has been exaggerated, concerned parties from outside the region have a role to play. If that role is to be constructive and pragmatic, it must be based upon the understanding that war is possible. Once that axiom has been accepted, the necessity of discussing the nature of deterrence with Pakistani interlocutors should be clear. All too often, the Pakistani leadership has heard foreign observers and academics echo their wishful thinking that somehow nuclear capabilities will compensate for their failures in other areas and console an electorate on the verge of despair. Convincing the Pakistani elite that they must be more realistic about the strengths and weaknesses of deterrence, and the resulting implications for their security policy, is imperative.

An important corollary of the conclusion that war is possible and deterrence should not be over-estimated is that Pakistan and its security partners must cautiously reconsider the nature of their support for the Kashmir insurgency. The message Islamabad receives from friendly Gulf states – particularly Saudi Arabia – will be of special importance on this issue. Pakistani leaders and their counterparts in other states should assess carefully the necessity of stoking the fires beneath the Kashmir uprising. Kashmir is not likely to be detached from the Indian state by force, and neither the *Ummah* nor the government of Pakistan requires such a separation for their legitimacy or well-being.

For arms suppliers, the continuing possibility of war in South Asia as highlighted in this analysis makes it imperative to consider the nuclear factor when selling conventional military technology. Hitherto, suppliers have neglected the nuclear factor, whether through indifference or a simple-minded belief that nuclear deterrence had created a stability that absolved them of responsibility for profitable, and therefore desirable, transactions. In fact, when it comes to air forces in nuclear South Asia, there really is no such thing as a conventional weapon any longer. Because of the strategically decisive nature of air power, and the counterforce and strategic defense capabilities inherent in conventional technologies used by air forces, any transfer of technology to a regional air force has implications for nuclear stability. Germany, the United Kingdom and the United States seem to have accepted this reality, albeit belatedly. But France, Israel and Russia apparently have not.[28]

While conventional arms transfers may have greater implications for nuclear stability and strategic balance than is often appreciated, the impact of some nominal nuclear systems should not be exaggerated. In the case of India, in particular, nuclear-capable ballistic missiles, such as the Agni 2, may be deployed during the next decade more out of pique with the United States and in the interests of bureaucratic prestige than any tangible military requirement. For this reason, it will be important for other parties – especially China – not to infer malign intent from Indian nuclear deployments that may otherwise appear provocative.

Taking a step back from the immediate concerns raised by military and nuclear capabilities as a grand strategy, it appears likely that Pakistan will remain dependent on foreign aid, if it is to avoid collapse. The same is no longer true for India, and foreign aid relationships with India should be reassessed. With the rapid growth made possible by economic liberalization the 1990s, India's economy is sufficiently large to fund programs for economic development and the alleviation of poverty.[29] If it chooses instead to spend the equivalent of US$3.4 billion on military research and development programs that make little contribution either to the economy or to national security (since none of the programs that responds to a formal military requirement has met it), that can be counted a failure of Indian democracy.[30] Aid donors can find needier recipients in Africa and Latin America, not to mention several of the less prosperous Islamic states.

Furthermore, India remains the key to regional peace and stability. In 1997, the region enjoyed a brief spell of détente as Delhi followed the Gujral doctrine and Pakistan responded favourably. If India and Pakistan are to avoid disaster, it will not be through reluctant participation in arms control and confidence-building measures, but through rapprochement. India must be encouraged to take the lead, whichever political party is leading the government. Goodwill from India can beget goodwill.

Concluding Remarks

A Gulf Perspective

This volume has focused on the changing balance-of-power equation resulting from nuclear detonations by India and Pakistan from the perspective of these two countries, as well as that of China, a key regional player. Through the lens of international politics, the effects of the blasts on the non-proliferation regime as well as the future strategic balance of forces in the region has been assessed. The events of May 1998, however, also have an enduring impact in a more indirect sense when it comes to the adjoining regions of South Asia. In particular, the Arabian Gulf, which for geographical, historic and strategic reasons, has felt this impact and needs to be drawn into the larger security discussions that have arisen. Specific attention must be paid to the questions of how the nuclear tests have affected the security situation in this volatile area, whether threat perceptions or regional ambitions have undergone serious reconsideration and what message was conveyed as a result of the events taking place in South Asia. With the Arabian Gulf representing one of the vital strategic regions of the world, these, in addition to other related and equally pertinent questions, deserve an answer.

That a correlation exists between events in South Asia and security in the Arabian Gulf should be self-evident. First, geographical proximity ensures that decisions of strategic significance taken on the subcontinent reverberate in policy-making circles throughout the Gulf region. Iran has a border with Pakistan; Oman and the United Arab Emirates (UAE) share a coastline with the Indian Ocean; and the weather patterns in both regions are closely linked. Second, there are the historical trade and economic links fostered over generations which now manifest themselves in the regular exchange of goods and services as well as in close personal and social ties. This has led to what can be labeled a civilizational relationship between the Gulf and South Asia. Today, the Gulf provides employment for many South Asian workers who, in turn, provide their services to the benefit and for the development of Gulf societies. Politically, the peoples of the Gulf identify not only with the Muslims of all of South Asia but also with the non-alignment strategy practiced by many of the states in this region which is seen as a continuation of the tradition of Arab nationalism as exemplified by Nasser.

From this perspective, it is clear that the Arabian Gulf region cannot remain indifferent to the events preoccupying the subcontinent. Neither can it play the role of a mere observer. The nuclear detonations exposed the fact that the Gulf is now directly linked to the human and environmental destruction that could result as part of a possible nuclear exchange. Even if such drastic circumstances do not arise, and their prevention must of course remain the highest priority, since threats to the continued economic and social well-being of the region persist. The potential for political conflict is ever-present and must be guarded against. There is a sense in the Gulf that to continue down the path of nuclear testing and possible proliferation of other Weapons of Mass Destruction (WMD) is playing with fire, and may result in uncontrollable consequences culminating in a self-fulfilling prophecy.

More specifically, the concerns that echo within the Gulf region are based on several factors. There is a latent worry about the future of Indo-Pakistani relations as a result of the historic rivalry that has persisted between these neighbors. Statements of peaceful intent are not sufficient to allay fears that either side will be tempted to launch a decisive first strike. This is a real possibility because of the short distances involved, the poor warning systems, the small stockpiles and the contentious issues, such as Kashmir, which all form part of the highly complex Indo-Pakistani nuclear relationship. Neither does Mutually Assured Destruction (MAD) ensure adequate restraint, and there is no room for complacency, especially in view of the lessons learned during the Cold War.

There are also nagging questions about the rationale for the tests, the answers to which remain vague and unsatisfactory to a large degree. While Pakistan's decision to proceed with testing was clearly a response, the Indian rationale is harder to understand. In some ways, it is seen as a way to evade the problems confronting its leadership and possibly a sign of an unwillingness to face reality. If its status as a great power is of concern to India, it should realize that such a standing is not solely measured in terms of warheads and missiles, in particular when a large proportion of its population suffers from severe economic and social dislocation. To argue, however, that there exists a mixture of an inferiority complex and political recklessness would be too simplistic. There can be no doubt that India faces some very real threats to its security, in addition to having valid reasons for being skeptical about unequal treatment it receives regarding nuclear issues from the traditional nuclear powers. India has always been at the forefront of advocating moves towards global nuclear disarmament, but their own tests have most certainly sent the wrong message about the utility of nuclear weapons. As a result, the two tendencies in Indian politics – the one based on the legacy of Mahatma Gandhi and the other espoused by today's Hindu nationalists – have further exposed the severe fragmentation of Indian society in the aftermath of the tests. In that sense, it may have been too easy to view the use of nuclear weapons as a tool for domestic political advantage, or to create an artificial feeling of unity based on fanaticism.

There are also problems further down the road. We have already witnessed the collapse of the Soviet Union as a result of the contradictions inherent in an arms race, and the legacy with which many of its successor states, most importantly Russia, are having to grapple is clearly visible. Furthermore, the costs of the nuclear tests do not cease with the event itself and thus the diversion of valuable resources from the goals of economic and social development is on-going, if not increasing. Such dislocation does not bode well for lasting political stability, neither does it add to a common security platform that can no longer be defined today in purely military terms. While South Asia has discovered the utility of economic growth strategies as a way forward, security strategy remains very much dominated by its political and military dimensions.

Apart from their effects on the direct relationship between India and Pakistan, the nuclear tests conveyed a message with numerous negative consequences for the Gulf region. At the outset, it is important to recognize that there is no such thing as an "Islamic bomb", in terms of a weapon that can single-handedly raise the Muslim world to great power status. In fact, its development dramatically increases the insecurity of all of its members. The Gulf provides a vivid example of the disruptive power of both conventional and non-conventional weapons. Iraq has proved that it is willing to use chemical weapons against its neighbors, having done so against the Iranians in their eight-year war as well as against its own population. It cannot be denied that any WMD weapon in the hands of someone like Saddam Hussein is a direct threat against the survival of the rest of the Gulf states.

Iran has demonstrated that it has no qualms about extending its hegemonic ambitions at the expense of its smaller southern neighbors, by taking part of their territory (the occupation of the UAE islands of Abu Musa and the Greater and Lesser Tunbs) as well as by interfering in their internal affairs and trying to spread its version of an Islamic revolution. Furthermore, due to the fact that the current Iranian military expansion program is far out of step with Iranian economic realities, the potential threat of Iranian actions against any of the Gulf state remains real. Iranian acquisition of nuclear weapons would have devastating consequences as has been shown by Iraq's example. Statements by Iranian leaders that atomic power is needed to create balance in the region are in this sense extremely misleading. Of course, it should not be forgotten that the latent Iranian–Pakistani rivalry could provide more incentives for the Iranians to speed up their nuclear program. All of this is complicated further by numerous reports of cooperation between India, Pakistan and various states of the region. Indications that Pakistan has sold Iraq enriched uranium in the past, which enabled Iraq to move forward in its nuclear program and of the collaboration at the nuclear level between Israel and India, Iran and India, not to mention the current exchanges taking place between Iran, Russia and China, are extremely disturbing.

Overall, it is the revival of a desire among several nations of the region to possess their own nuclear weapons that, over the long run, is the most serious consequence of the nuclear explosions. The nuclear tests have demonstrated that even relatively poor countries have the means to build nuclear weapons, and that if a country with the basic scientific and technological infrastructure to build a bomb decides to go nuclear, it is extremely difficult to prevent it from doing so. Equally daunting is the new hallmark that has been established, that the mark of a true regional power is its possession of nuclear weapons. Statements by Iran that the testing of its Shehab-3 missile, a nuclear capable missile with a range of 1,300 km, in July 1988, was a response to the South Asian tests as well as to Pakistan's testing of its Ghauri intermediate-range missile in April 1998, are an indication of this perception.

What is the future course of action? Are there some concrete steps that can be taken by the Gulf states to prevent some of the negative consequences of nuclear proliferation from manifesting themselves? For one thing, there is urgent need to break out of the cycle of mutual deterrence and balance of forces that has engulfed both India and Pakistan as well as the Gulf region. A clear demonstration of displeasure about the testing itself and the messages that it conveyed should be expressed. Economic sanctions do very little to solve the strategic dilemma that has been created – in fact, they may exacerbate the situation by leading to further economic and social decline and resulting in instability. Iraq is the most vivid example of how sanctions have destroyed the very basic fabric of society without doing any damage to its leadership. Sanctions are too often used as a convenient tool to avoid confronting the real issues. Instead, the problem of proliferation needs to be discussed openly and frankly and brought to the attention of the highest levels of regional and international organizations, in order to allow as broad a cooperation as possible.

The nuclear detonations also focused the debate on the need for a zone free of WMD in the Middle East. There should be a ban on all types of WMD in the Middle East with all states taking equal responsibility and building adequate control mechanisms to ensure compliance, as well as qualitative and quantitative asymmetry in the military potential of all the states. A regional conference under the aegis of the United Nations might prove useful in fostering the debate about setting up a regional center for considering problems of non-proliferation and the peaceful use of atomic energy. While there is certainly a need to focus on the elimination of Israel's nuclear program (it is now the only undeclared nuclear state in the world), it is also important not to make security in the Gulf contingent on Israeli compliance. In fact, a positive step in the direction of disarmament might potentially be useful as a means to pressurize the Israelis to reign in their own program instead of giving them reasons to further their efforts. In this respect, the Gulf is unique, and solely responsible for establishing security in its sphere of influence. A WMD-free zone treaty, such as the one established by the Pelindaba treaty in April 1996 and now signed by more than 50 African states, is a very worthwhile consideration.

Whatever immediate steps are taken, there is a need for further analysis, frequent meetings and extensive discussions at all levels of decision- and policy-making. It is only through an extensive effort by all those concerned with safeguarding the security of the Arabian Gulf, that the negative impact of the ominous events of May 1998 can be countered and ultimately eliminated. It is hoped that the present volume has made a worthwhile contribution to that aspiration.

Contributors

ERIC ARNETT

Dr. Eric Arnett is the Leader of the Project on Military Technology at the Stockholm International Peace Research Institute (SIPRI), where he has worked since 1992. Previously, he was a Senior Program Associate of the American Association for the Advancement of Science's Program on Science and International Security and Director of the Program's Project on Advanced Weaponry in the Developing World. He has a PhD from Carnegie Mellon University's Department of Engineering and Public Policy (US) and a BS from Cornell University's Sibley School of Mechanical and Aerospace Engineering (US) . His numerous publications include chapters in four recent SIPRI studies: *Nuclear Weapons and Arms Control in South Asia after the Test Ban* (1998); *Military Capacity and the Risk of War: China, India, Pakistan and Iran* (1997); *Nuclear Weapons After the Comprehensive Test Ban: Implications for Modernization and Proliferation* (1995) and *Implementing the Comprehensive Test Ban: New Aspects of Definition, Organization and Verification* (1994).

CHRISTIAN KOCH

Dr. Christian Koch is a Senior Researcher at the Emirates Center for Strategic Studies and Research in Abu Dhabi, United Arab Emirates. His areas of focus are the political and strategic developments that affect the security environment of the Arab Gulf region and its adjoining areas. Dr. Koch received his PhD from the University of Erlangen-Nürnberg in Germany and his MA from the School of International Service, American University, Washington, DC. He is the co-editor, with David Long, of the ECSSR publication *Gulf Security in the Twenty-First Century* (1997).

MICHAEL KREPON

Mr. Michael Krepon is President of the Henry L. Stimson Center, a non-profit, non-partisan institution founded in 1989, specializing in arms control and international security issues. His areas of interest are the phased reduction and elimination of weapons of mass destruction and the utilization of confidence-building measures to alleviate tensions and promote reconciliation, particularly in South Asia. Mr. Krepon graduated from Franklin and Marshall College and The Johns Hopkins School of Advanced and International Studies. He is the author of *Arms Control in the Reagan Administration* (1989) published by the University Press of America; *Strategic Stalemate, Nuclear Weapons and Arms Control in American Politics* (1984); and co-editor of *Crisis Prevention, Confidence Building, and Reconciliation in South Asia* (1995); *Open Skies, Arms Control and Cooperative Security* (1992); and *The Politics of Arms Control Treaty Ratification* (1991). Krepon's latest book, "Global Confidence Building: Tools for Troubled Regions" is due to be published shortly by St. Martin's Press and Macmillan, which have also published his other books.

NAJAM RAFIQUE

Mr. Najam Rafique is a Senior Research Fellow at the Institute of Strategic Studies in Islamabad, Pakistan and Deputy Editor of the quarterly journals *Strategic Studies* and *Strategic Perspectives*, published by the Institute of Strategic Studies. His research interests focus on US foreign policy and politics in South Asia. Prior to joining the Institute for Strategic Studies, Mr. Rafique worked as an Assistant Editor of the Paper Printing and Packaging Company and as Sub-Editor of the *Muslim Daily*. He earned an MS in Political Science from the University of Illinois at Urbana-Champaign (US), an MSc in Defense and Strategic Studies from Quaid-i-Azam University and a BA from the University of Punjab.

JASJIT SINGH

Air Commodore Jasjit Singh, AVSM, VrC, VM, IAF (retd), is the former Director of Operations of the Indian Air Force. Since 1987, he has been Director of the Institute for Defence Studies and Analyses, New Delhi. Air Commodore Singh is also a Consultant to the Standing Committee of Defence of the Parliament; Adviser to the Finance Commission of India; and Member of the National Security Advisory Board. In 1990–91, he served as a Member of the International Commission for a New Asia. Air Commodore Singh has written extensively on strategic and security issues and is the author and editor of more than two dozen books, including *Air Power in Modern Warfare* (1985), *Non-provocative Defence* (1989), both published by Lancers International, New Delhi, and *Nuclear India* (1998) published by Knowledge World, New Delhi.

MARVIN G. WEINBAUM

Dr. Marvin G. Weinbaum is Professor Emeritus of Political Science at the University of Illinois at Urbana-Champaign, and currently Scholar-in-Residence at the Middle East Institute in Washington, DC. He is also an Adjunct Professor at George Washington University (US). Professor Weinbaum earned a PhD from Columbia University in 1965, and joined the Illinois faculty in the same year. At Illinois, he served for 15 years as the director of the Program in South Asian and Middle Eastern Studies. He was a senior fellow at the United States Institute of Peace in 1996–97, and has held Fulbright Research Fellowships for Egypt in 1981–82 and Afghanistan in 1989–90. Dr. Weinbaum is the author or editor of six books the more recent of these being *South Asia Approaches the Millennium: Reexamining National Security* (1995), co-edited with Chetan Kumar and *Afghanistan and Pakistan: Resistance and Reconstruction* (1994), authored by him. Both books have been published by Westview Press, Boulder, Colorado.

Notes

1

THE LIMITS OF *REALPOLITIK* IN THE SECURITY
ENVIRONMENT OF SOUTH ASIA

1 For a discussion see Robert Gilpin, *War and Change in World Politics* (New York, NY: Cambridge University Press, 1981), 28–29.

2 Rajesh Basrur, "South Asia's Persistent Cold War, an *ACDIS Occasional Paper* (Champaign, IL: Program in Arms Control, Disarmament, and International Security, University of Illinois, November 1996), 2.

3 C. Rammanohar Reddy, "The Wages of Armageddon III" *The Hindu*, September 2, 1998. In an extensive examination of costs, Reddy points out that one Agni missile can finance the annual operations of 13,000 primary health care centers.

4 It is believed to have taken the United States and Soviet Union some 15 years. Steven Erlanger, "India's Arms Race Isn't Safe Like the Cold War," *The New York Times*, July 12, 1998.

5 Ejaz Haider, "A Pyrrhic Victory?" *The Friday Times* (Lahore), August 14, 1998, 7.

6 See "Mahbub ul-Haq," *The Economist*, July 25, 1998, 84.

7 Darryl D'Monte, "Dangerous Changes: India's Nuclear Mistake," *The New Leader*, June 1–15, 1998, 7.

8 As Thomas Thorton has written in arguing that Pakistan's relationship with India calls for reassessment: "Nuclear stalemate may seem reassuring compared to the security deficit of 1947, but it is a defensive and sterile policy that probably responds to a misinterpretation of Indian intentions, now if not then. Single-minded preoccupation with the subcontinental rivalry overtaxes Pakistan's diplomatic and security capabilities. The economic costs are crushing." Thomas P. Thorton, "Fifty Years of Insecurity," A paper prepared for the Conference to Commemorate the 50th Anniversary of India's and Pakistan's Independence, The Woodrow Wilson Center, Washington, DC, June 4, 1997, 20.

9 Robert Cooper, "The Post-Modern State and the World Order," *The Economist*, December 20, 1997, 41.

2

NUCLEARIZATION AND REGIONAL SECURITY:
AN INDIAN PERSPECTIVE

1 The Indian state of Arunachal Pradesh, which elects members to the Indian parliament, is as large as Taiwan and continues to be shown on Chinese maps as

Chinese territory, in spite of a 40-year-old promise by China to revise what it termed as the old "imperial maps". In the Northwest, China has occupied 18,500 square miles of territory in Aksai Chin since the early 1950s. Agreements to demarcate a "Line of Actual Control" between the two countries have not yet produced concrete results, in spite of the 1993 and 1996 agreements.

2 There is a view that the international order is multipolar. But multipolarity still signifies the existence of poles and spheres of control and influence. Polycentricity, on the other hand, implies non-hegemonic relationships among sovereign states. More important, multipolarity would require the major powers in the system to possess almost equal capabilities.

3 The United States, by virtue of its global interests and strategy of engagement in Asia, will continue to be an 'Asian' power for the foreseeable future.

4 Quoted in Bill Gertz, "General Who Threatened L. A. Tours US on China Mission," *Washington Times,* December 18, 1996, 6.

5 US nuclear non-proliferation policy was encapsulated in this imperative, which was to apply to South Asia. But since Pakistan has traditionally mortgaged its own policy to actions by India, it became applicable essentially to India.

6 Dr. William Perry, in a speech at the Foreign Policy Association, New York, January 31, 1995.

7 For a partial account of the negotiations for security guarantees, see recently declassified US documents under the title of *National Security Archive Electronic Book No.6: India and Pakistan - On the Nuclear Threshold* by Joyce Battle, 1998.

8 General Khalid Mahmud Arif, *Working with Zia: Pakistan's Power Politics 1977-1988* (Karachi: Oxford University Press, 1995), 431.

9 Ibid., 434.

10 A Majority Report of the International Security, Proliferation, and Federal Services Subcommittee, *China: The Proliferation Primer* (Washington, DC: United States Senate Committee on Government Affairs, January 1998).

11 Agha Shahi, in Fasahat H. Syed (ed.) *Nuclear Disarmament and Conventional Arms Control Including Light Weapons* (Rawalpindi: FRIENDS, 1997), 421.

12 General Aslam Beg (who headed the Pakistan Army during 1988-91) in Fasahat H. Syed, ibid. See also his statement at the Henry Stimson Center, Washington, DC, July 1995.

13 See interview by the Chief of Army Staff, Indian Army, General VN Sharma to K Subrahmanyam, "It's all bluff and bluster," *Economic Times,* May 18, 1993, 7.

14 In fact most of the armed violence and militancy in South Asia and around it is confined to small areas contiguous to international borders. See Jasjit Singh, "Light Weapons and Conflict in Southern Asia" in Jasjit Singh (ed.) *Light Weapons and International Security* (Pugwash: IDSA and New Delhi: BASIC, 1995), 50-62.

15 *China: The Proliferation Primer*, op. cit.

3

PAKISTAN AND REGIONAL SECURITY IN SOUTH ASIA

1 References to "heavy agenda" and "external alliances" are terms familiar to academics who have been studying India-Pakistan relations. It is possible to

quote examples such as lack of progress in making the South Asian Association for Regional Cooperation (SAARC) into a viable entity in order to alleviate the real issues confronting South Asia: eradication of poverty, hunger, illiteracy, provision of basic medical care and decent housing, access to clean drinking water, cooperation on human rights issues such as women's rights and child labour. These are issues of the "heavy agenda". However, they have been given very little importance, if not totally ignored, compared to the issues of Kashmir which both countries quote as being a major hindrance, preventing meaningful cooperation on other issues. Kashmir itself provides the two countries with a pretext to pursue military programmes which require both countries to commit over half their annual budgets on defence and military sales from countries like the US, Russia, Germany, France, Sweden and China. The 1998 defence budget allocations include: $9.9 billion for India and $3.2 billion for Pakistan. (Quoted in *The Economist*, May 22, 1999, in a Survey on India and Pakistan, p. 6). More so in the case of India which has only recently made major contracts with Russia for the sale of tanks, nuclear submarines, and Theatre Missile Defence (TDM) systems. (For an excellent article on sale of TDMs to India, see Gregory Koblentz, "Viewpoint: Theatre Missile Defence and South Asia: A Volatile Mix," *The Nonproliferation Review*, vol. 4, no. 3, Spring/Summer, 1997. (http://cns.miis.edu/pubs/npr/koblen43.htm).

2 Mahnaz Ispahani, "Pakistan: Dimensions of Insecurity," *Adelphi Papers* no. 246 (London: IISS, 1990), 30.

3 "US Claims progress in Nuclear Dialogue With Pakistan", from Washington correspondent of *The Nation*, January 23, 1999. Also see "Pakistan, US Officials to Discuss 5-point Agenda", News Network International (NNI), Islamabad, *News*, January 25, 1999.

4 The P-5 grouping includes: US, Russia, Britain, France and China. The G-8 includes: US, Russia, France, Britain, Germany, Italy, Canada and Japan.

5 See Eric Arnett (ed.) "Nuclear Weapons and Arms Control in South Asia after the Test Ban, *SIPRI Research Report* no. 14 (New York, NY: Oxford University Press, 1998), 6.

6 Rajesh Rajagopalan, "Nuclear Weapons in South Asia," (Washington, DC: India Abroad Center for Political Awareness, December 1996).

7 Ibid.

8 *DAWN*, August 19, 1997.

9 "Chemical Weapons Convention: Under Scrutiny," Manoj Joshi, *India Today*, New Delhi, May 31, 1997, 90–92.

10 Lt. Gen Kamal Matinuddin, "Nuclearization of South Asia: Implications and Prospects," *Regional Studies* vol. 16, no. 3 (Summer 1998): 21.

11 See "India Ready to Develop Nuclear Bombs: Atomic Experts," *News*, March 5, 1998. Also see "BJP and Indian Nuclear Option," Umer Farooq, News Analysis, *The Nation*, March 6, 1999, "Policy Document of BJP on Nuclear Issue," extracts, S. Iftikhar Gilani, *The Nation*, March 8, 1999.

4

CHINA AND REGIONAL SECURITY IN SOUTH ASIA

1   See, for example, the discussion in *Foreign Affairs Magazine* about the "China Threat", including Richard Bernstein and Ross H. Munro, "The Coming Conflict with America," *Foreign Affairs* vol. 76, no. 2 (March/April 1997): 18-32; Robert S. Ross, "Enter the Dragon," *Foreign Policy* no. 104 (Fall 1996): 18-25; and John J. Schulz, "China as a Strategic Threat: Myths and Verities," *Strategic Review* vol. 26, no. 1 (Winter 1998): 5-16.

2   Samuel S. Kim, "China as a Great Power," *Current History* vol. 96, no. 611 (September 1997): 246-251. Kim states that ". . . in an era of globalization, power needs to be seen in synthetic terms. The traditional military and strategic concept of power pays too much attention to the state's aggregate power . . . and too little to the more dynamic and interdependent notions of power in an issue-specific domain – that is, power defined in terms of control over outcomes."

3   There are projections that in the next 10 to 15 years, China could surpass the United States in terms of total economy. See, William Overholt, *The Rise of China* (New York, NY: Norton, 1993) and the study by the RAND Corporation, *Long-Term Economic and Military Trends, 1994-2015: The United States and Asia*, edited by Charles Wolf, Jr. (Santa Monica, CA: RAND Corporation, 1995), 5-8. It has to be remembered, however, that these projections assume a continued growth rate above the 10 percent level for the next 15 years, a development that is highly unrealistic.

4   *The Economist*, October 24, 1998, 23.

5   "China's Evolving Maritime Strategy," Parts 1 & 2, *Jane's Intelligence Review* vol. 8, no. 3 & 4 (March & April 1996): 129-133 and 186-191 respectively. See also, Ehsan Ahrari, "China's Naval Forces Look to Extend their Blue-water Reach," *Jane's Intelligence Review* vol. 10, no. 4 (April 1998): 31-36.

6   Joseph S. Nye, "China's Re-emergence and the Future of the Asia-Pacific," *Survival* vol. 39, no. 4 (Winter 1997-98): 68-70.

7   In July 1998, China released its first ever Defense White Paper which focused on the development of a new security concept. In it, China argued for the establishment of five principles for peaceful coexistence – mutual respect for territorial integrity and sovereignty, mutual non-aggression, non-interference in each other's internal affairs, equality, mutual benefit and peaceful coexistence – the need for open markets to promote economic growth, strengthening multilateral institutions, and the formation of strategic partnerships. Overall, China has begun to link economic development to its political and military security.

8   Kim, op. cit., 251. See also the October 24, 1998 issue of *The Economist*, which takes a largely pessimistic view of China's near-term potential when asking the question "Is China Next?" in terms of the Asian economic contagion, or the more positive assessment of recent Chinese reforms by Georg Blume entitled "Hauptsache, die Katze Fängt Mäuse," *Die Zeit*, October 22, 1998, 37.

9   Anoushiravan Ehteshami, "The Changing Balance of Power in Asia," *The Emirates Occasional Papers* no. 16 (Abu Dhabi: The Emirates Center for Strategic Studies and Research, 1998), 2.

10 Ibid., 3

11 Richard N. Rosecrance, "Bipolarity, Multipolarity and the Future," in James N. Rosenau (ed.) *International Politics and Foreign Policy: A Reader in Research and Theory* (New York, NY: The Free Press, 1969): 329.

12 Trevor Findlay, "Development of the Asia-Pacific Security Regime," Presentation to the second Stockholm International Peace Research Institute (SIPRI) Middle East Workshop, Stockholm, May 1997, 1. See also, Sheldon W. Simon, "Security prospects in Southeast Asia: collaborative efforts and the ASEAN Regional Forum," *The Pacific Review* vol. 11, no. 2 (1998): 195-212. With the concern in the region about China shifting from economic development (once achieved) to strategic consolidation rising, ASEAN is seen as a way to counter increasing Chinese influence.

13 See, for example, the discussion in Yong Deng, "The Chinese Conception of National Interests in International Relations," *The China Quarterly* no. 154 (June 1998): especially 311-316.

14 See Steven Hoffmann, "The International Politics of Southern Asia," in James Sperling, Yogendra Malik and David Louscher (eds.) *Zones of Amity, Zones of Enmity: The Prospects for Economic and Military Security in Asia* (Leiden: E.J. Brill, 1998): 46-47.

15 This objective needs, of course, to be separated from the broader national security imperatives that make up China's overall strategy. Among the fundamental objectives included here, they are (1) to safeguard China's national territorial integrity and sovereignty; (2) to oversee and promote national construction and social development, (3) to build up elements of national power; and (4) to ensure continued national prosperity. For further discussion, see Pan Shiying, *Reflections on Modern Strategy: Post-Cold War Strategic Theory* (Beijing: Shijie Zhishi Chubanshe, 1993).

16 See Ehsan Ahrari, "South Asia Faces the Future with a Clean Strategic Slate," *Jane's Intelligence Review* vol. 10, no. 12 (December 1998): 33.

17 Robert S. Ross, "Beijing as a Conservative Power," *Foreign Affairs* vol. 76, no. 2 (March/April 1997): 33-44.

18 It was, for example, from Pakistan that former US Secretary of State Henry Kissinger launched his secret visit to China in 1971, which paved the way for the historic visit of US President Richard Nixon to Beijing in the following year.

19 Ahmed Rashid, "Ein neuer globaler Ölmulti: Chinas strategische Rolle in Zentralasien," *Internationale Politik* vol. 53, no. 3 (March 1998): 29-31.

20 Xing, Guangcheng, "Security Issues in China's Relations with Central Asian States," in Yongjin Zhang and Rouben Azizian (ed.) *Ethnic Challenges beyond Borders: Chinese and Russian Perspectives of the Central Asian Conundrum* (London: Macmillan Press Ltd., 1998 in association with St. Anthony's College), 207-213. For another discussion about the emerging relationship between the People's Republic of China and some of the Central Asian states see Yasmin Melet, "China's political and economic relations with Kazakhstan and Kyrgystan," *Central Asian Survey* vol. 17, no. 2 (1998): 229-252.

21 "Taliban Train Muslim Separatists for Terrorism in China," *The Telegraph*, October 4, 1998.

22 "The Changing Face of China," *Jane's Defence Weekly*, December 16, 1998: 21.

23 J. Mohan Malik, "India Goes Nuclear: Rationale, Benefits, Costs and Implications," *Contemporary Southeast Asia* vol. 20, no. 2 (August 1998): 194.

24 Gary Klintworth, "Chinese Perspectives on India as a Great Power," in Ross Babbage and Sandy Gordon (ed.) *India's Strategic Future: Regional State or Global Power?* (London: Macmillan Press Ltd., 1992), 96.

25 Cited in Dorothy Woodman, *Himalayan Frontiers* (London: Cresset Press, 1969), 228. In 1954, in fact, India and China signed a treaty concerning the status of Tibet, named the "Five Principles of Peaceful Co-Existence." While not mentioning the boundary problem between the two countries, India referred to the "Tibet region of China" throughout the 1950s. See Mahinda Werake, "China and South Asia: Some Historical Perspectives," in Shelton U. Kodikara (ed.) *South Asian Strategic Issues: Sri Lankan Perspectives* (New Delhi: Sage Publications, 1991), 57-59.

26 For a study on the border war see Xuecheng Liu, *The Sino-Indian Border Dispute and Sino-Indian Relations* (New York, NY: University Press of America, 1994).

27 One claim has it that 90 percent of Chinese arms sales go to countries that border India. See Malik, op.cit., 195.

28 Malik, ibid., 197.

29 See, for example, Andrew J. Nathan and Robert S. Ross, *The Great Wall and the Empty Fortress: China's Search for Security* (New York, NY: W.W. Norton & Co., 1997), 118-122.

30 Looked at from this perspective, then, the claim that China was the precipitating factor in the decision by India to go ahead with its nuclear tests is rather misleading. Rather, from this point of view, the case becomes one of a weak government in a weak state that was desperate for some domestic success and decided to utilize the one issue on which almost everyone could agree.

31 The extent of China's involvement in the development of the Pakistani nuclear program has been well documented. See, for example, the chapter on Pakistan in Rodney W. Jones, Mark G. McDonough, Toby F. Dalto and Gregory D. Koblentz (eds) *Tracking Nuclear Proliferation 1998* (Washington, DC: Carnegie Endowment for International Peace, July 1998), or the NCI Issue Brief prepared by the Nuclear Control Institute, authored by Steven Dolley, *China's Non-Proliferation Words vs. China's Nuclear Proliferation Deeds* (available on the Institute's web site, http://www.nci.org).

32 "Burma Slides Under China's Shadow," *Jane's Intelligence Review* vol. 9, no. 6 (July 1997): 320-25.

33 This is an argument repeated by Malik, op. cit., who states that China has increased its troop presence in Tibet from 100,000 to 400,000, as well as building an extension of an airfield runaway in order to handle Chinese Su-27 fighters. For the statement by Defense Minister Fernandez, see "India Defense Minister says China a Threat," *Reuters*, May 18, 1998.

34 This is a common argument that has been picked up by a number of scholars. In his recent article, J. Mohan Malik writes: "China was in fact the most important actor to induce India to exercise its nuclear option. India's nuclear and missile capabilities owe much to the dynamics of the Sino-Indian rivalry. It is the adversarial nature of the Sino-Indian relationship which has driven the Indian, and, in turn, the Pakistani nuclear weapons program." See J. Mohan Malik, op. cit., 193.

35 Avery Goldstein, "Great Expectations: Interpreting China's Arrival," *International Security* vol. 22, no. 3 (Winter 1997/98): 42-54; Ikuo Kayahara, "China as a Military Power in the Twenty-first Century," *Japan Review of International Affairs*

vol. 12, no. 1 (Spring 1998): especially 56-60; Paul H.B. Gordon, "Uncertainty, Insecurity, and China's Military Power," *Current History* vol. 96, no. 611 (September 1997): 252-257.

36 "China's Evolving Maritime Strategy: Part 1 & 2," *Jane's Intelligence Review* vol. 8, no. 3 & 4 (March and April 1996): 129-133 and 186-191 respectively; Swaran Singh, "China's Changing Maritime Strategy: Implications for the Indian Ocean Region," *Journal for Indian Ocean Studies* vol. 5, no.1 (November 1997): 1-12; "China's Naval Forces Look to Extend their Blue-water Reach," *Jane's Intelligence Review* vol. 10, no. 4 (April 1998): 31-36.

37 "Security: The Race is On," *Far Eastern Economic Review*, June 11, 1998.

38 "China Pledge to Halt Nuke Aid to Pakistan - Albright," *Reuters*, June 28, 1998.

39 See the testimony by Paul Leventhal, President of the Nuclear Control Institute, in front of the Subcommittee on Telecommunications, Trade and Consumer Protection of the US House of Representatives, May 14, 1998 (Nuclear Control Institute website at http://www.nci.org)

40 As reported in the *International Herald Tribune*, May 29, 1998, 4.

41 "Russia, China Say Worried by Asian Nuclear Tests," *Reuters*, July 3, 1998.

42 "China's Response to India could Boost its Reputation," *Washington Post*, May 15, 1998.

43 "Jiang Bars Nuclear Blasts," *International Herald Tribune*, June 4, 1998.

44 "Remarks by the President on US-China Relations in the 21st Century," given to the National Geographic Society, June 11, 1998 (White House website at http://www.whitehouse.gov)

45 "Full Text – China/US Summit Statement on South Asia," *Reuters*, June 27, 1998.

46 "India blasts China-US Summit call on South Asia," *Reuters*, June 28, 1998.

5

THE FUTURE STRATEGIC BALANCE IN SOUTH ASIA

1 On the misapplication of Islam to science during the Zia years, see Pervez Hoodbhoy, *Islam and Science: Islamic Orthodoxy and the Battle for Rationality* (London: Zed Books Ltd, 1991).

2 In a limited war in which Pakistan used tactical nuclear weapons selectively, the Indian Army's performance would be degraded in the areas successfully attacked with nuclear weapons. The Indian Air Force could still achieve other war aims, as could the Army when operating in sectors in which nuclear weapons had not been used. Such selective use of tactical nuclear weapons may be the most likely scenario of nuclear use, since it would keep the number of civilian casualties to a minimum and might be perceived by Pakistani planners as leaving the onus for escalation to strategic nuclear use on India. Such an approach is advocated by Syed Anwar Mehdi, "Nuclear Ambivalence Versus a Well-Defined Policy Involving Minimum Political Fallout," *The Citadel*, summer 1994.

3 So reports Stephen P. Cohen after interviews in 1980. Stephen P. Cohen, *The Pakistan Army* (London: University of California Press, 1984), 153.

4 Hamish McDonald, "Destroyer of Worlds," *Far East Economic Review*, April 30, 1992, 24.

5 Gujral told the respected journalist Shekhar Gupta. Shekar Gupta, "Nuclear Weapons in the Subcontinent," in Michael Krepon (ed.) *Defense and Insecurity in Southern Asia* (Washington, DC: Henry L. Stimson Center, 1995), 40.

6 Former Pakistani Chief of Army Staff General Mirza Aslam Beg said in 1998 that the ability to deliver nuclear weapons by aircraft was achieved late in 1990, several months after the Kashmir crisis of the previous spring. Ahmed Rashid and Shiraz Sidhva, "Might and Menace," *Far East Economic Review*, June 4, 1998, 34.

7 Pakistan Television, Address to the nation by Prime Minister Mohammad Nawaz Sharif, May 28, 1998, in FBIS-NES-98-148.

8 Asad Durrani, "Our Friend, the Enemy," *News*, June 11, 1998. As director of ISI, Durrani was responsible for Pakistani support to the Kashmir insurgency.

9 Tactical missiles could be used against massed Indian armor in the Rajasthan desert, even if Pakistan loses the air battle. Pakistani military planners say they have studied attack options that would confine the nuclear effects to the immediate vicinity while inflicting high military casualties.

10 When this author has expressed his skepticism about Pakistan's willingness to actually follow through on its threat of first use, he has been consistently assured by Pakistani military colleagues that there is no doubt as to their commitment to use nuclear weapons early in war.

11 Several recent studies of Indian nuclear policy have fallen into error by making the assumption that the decision to test in 1974 was the same as the decision to acquire a nuclear weapon option (apparently made in 1971), or the decision to acquire a deliverable weapon (only realized in 1990).

12 D. K. Palit and P. K. S. Namboodiri, *Pakistan's Islamic Bomb* (New Delhi: Vikas, 1979), 117. Palit, a hero of the 1962 war, was Commandant of the Indian Military Academy.

13 R. Prabhu, "US Targeting Indian High-Tech Capability: P. K. Iyengar," *Indian Express*, May 12, 1994.

14 Raja Ramanna, "We Have Enough Plutonium," *India Today*, September 15, 1994, 53. Iyengar and Ramanna may have been goading Pakistan into testing, which would have created an opportunity for India to test before signing the Comprehensive Test Ban Treaty without suffering such strong criticism. Pakistan withstood the temptation in 1994, but similar jibes in 1998 were among the factors that drove Pakistan to test after India had created a political opportunity by testing first.

15 P. R. Chari, *Indo-Pak Nuclear Standoff: The Role of the United States* (New Delhi: Manohar, 1995), 112-15, 127; and P. R. Chari, "Pakistan's Bomb: a Strategy of Deterrence Crafted on Make Believe," *Indian Express*, August 28, 1994.

16 V. N. Sharma, "It's All Bluff and Bluster," *Economic Times*, May 18, 1993.

17 Shekar Gupta and W. P. S. Sidhu, "The End Game Option," *India Today*, April 30, 1993.

18 The trend in Indian funding for military R&D is summarized in Eric Arnett, "Military Research and Development," in the *SIPRI Yearbook 1998* (Oxford: Oxford University Press, 1998). (More recent information is available in a usable form at the website http://www.sipri.se/projects/tech.html.)

19 This is the view of Air Commodore Jasjit Singh (ret.), who developed the concept of recessed deterrence and has been influential in the current government as part of the task force on the creation of a National Security Council. Jasjit

Singh, "A Nuclear Strategy for India," in Jasjit Singh (ed.) *Nuclear India* (New Delhi: Knowledge World, 1998), 314-324; and Jasjit Singh, "Defence: Budgeting for Security Needs," *Frontline*, July 18-31, 1998. See also Singh's remarks in Kenneth J. Cooper, "Nuclear Dilemmas: Vital Issues Face India as a Nuclear Power," *Washington Post*, May 25, 1998, A1.

20 By this I mean that the conventional forces are more important than the nuclear capabilities, not that conventional and nuclear military capabilities are strategically more important than India's economic and political advantages.

21 "Nukes Keep Pakistan Away, Says Indian Army Chief," *Dawn*, November 30, 1998.

22 Laser-guided bombs and related technology were delivered by France, Israel, Russia, the UK and the USA, starting in the early 1990s. Eric Arnett, "Conventional Arms Transfers and Nuclear Stability in South Asia," in Eric Arnett (ed.) *Nuclear Weapons and Arms Control in South Asia after the Test Ban* (Oxford: Oxford University Press, 1998), 79-81. A Russo-Israeli AWAC system is being developed for China and India. Barbara Opall-Rome, "Israel, US Lock Horns over Transfers to India," *Defense News*, November 2-8, 1998, 19.

23 In 1995, Bruce O. Riedel, the Deputy Assistant Secretary of Defense for Near Eastern and South Asian Affairs, told Congress, "US-Indian defense ties are better now than at any time in the past 30 years." US House of Representatives, Committee on International Relations, *US Interests in South Asia* (Washington, DC: US Government Printing Office, 1997), 96.

24 Pakistan's nuclear-capable ballistic missiles are thought to be stored at the Sargodha air base.

25 "No Chance of India-Pakistan Nuclear War," *Dawn*, March 22, 1998.

26 *News*, June 6, 1998.

27 Asad Durrani, "Pakistan's Nuclear Card," *Defence Journal*, June 1998. See also the view of Lt-Gen. Talat Masood (ret.), "If conventional strength, particularly the air arm and surveillance networks, continues to decrease . . . then the nuclear capability can be neutralized by preemptive conventional surgical strikes." Talat Masood, "Evolving a Correct Nuclear Posture," *Dawn*, August 21, 1998.

28 An important exception to this observation is the tacit policy described to the author by a Russian official to the effect that anti-radar missiles (ARMs) that could knock out the Pakistani warning network would not be sold to India. IAF officials say that India had no ARMs as of late 1997.

29 This is not to say that India should be punished economically for its nuclear tests. While the tests violated a global norm, India's other nuclear policies are generally supportive of norms that should be strengthened (in contrast with Pakistan's nuclear policies, which challenge norms to an extent that is not always appreciated).

30 India's budget for military R&D in 1998-99 is about Rs30 billion, an amount that has the purchasing power of US$3.4 billion in the US economy. In terms of foreign exchange, it is worth about US$820 million. For a discussion of the failure of democratically elected officials and parliamentarians properly to oversee the activities of the DRDO, see Ravinder Pal Singh, "India," in Ravinder Pal Singh (ed.) *Arms Procurement Decision Making, Volume I: China, India, Israel, Japan, South Korea and Thailand* (Oxford: Oxford University Press, 1998).

Bibliography

Ahrari, Ehsan. "Sino-Indian Nuclear Perspectives: So Close, Yet So Far Apart." *Jane's Intelligence Review* (August 1998).

—"China's Naval Forces Look to Extend their Blue-water Reach." *Jane's Intelligence Review* (April 1998).

—(ed.) *Military Capacity and the Risk of War: China, India, Pakistan and Iran* (Oxford: Oxford University Press, 1997).

—"Military Research and Development" in *SIPRI Yearbook 1996-1999* (Oxford: Oxford University Press, 1996-99).

—"Military Technology: the Case of India" in *SIPRI Yearbook 1994* (Oxford: Oxford University Press, 1994).

—(ed.) *Nuclear Weapons and Arms Control in South Asia after the Test Ban* (Oxford: Oxford University Press, 1998).

—(ed.) *Nuclear Weapons after the Comprehensive Test Ban: Implications for Modernization and Proliferation* (Oxford: Oxford University Press, 1996).

Arif, General Khalid Mahmud. *Working with Zia: Pakistan's Power Politics 1977-1988* (Karachi: Oxford University Press, 1995).

Ayoob, Mohammad. *India and Southeast Asia: Indian Perceptions and Policies* (London: Routledge, 1990, Published under the auspices of the Institute for Southeast Asian Studies, Singapore).

Babbage, Ross and Sandy Gordon (eds) *India's Strategic Future: Regional State or Global Power?* (London: Macmillan Press, 1992).

—*India's Strategic Future: Regional State or Global Power?* (New York, NY: St. Martin's Press, 1992).

Bajpai, Kanti and Stephen P. Cohen (eds) *South Asia After the Cold War* (Boulder, CO: Westview Press, 1993).

Bajwa, Farooq Naseem. *Pakistan and the West: The First Decade 1947-1957* (New York, NY: Oxford University Press, 1996).

Barnds, W. J. *India, Pakistan and the Great Powers* (New York, NY: Praeger, 1972).

Bernstein, Richard and Ross H. Munro. *The Coming Conflict with China* (New York, NY: Alfred A. Knopf, 1997).

Binnendijk, Hans and Ronald Montaperto. *Strategic Trends in China* (Washington, DC: National Defense University Press, 1998).

Bristow, Damon. "Mutual Mistrust Still Hampering Sino-Indian Rapprochement." *Jane's Intelligence Review* (August 1997).

Brookings Institution and the Council on Foreign Relations. *After the Test: US Policy Toward India and Pakistan* (New York, NY: Council on Foreign Relations Press, 1998).

Burke, S. M. *Pakistan's Foreign Policy* (New York, NY: Oxford University Press, 1973).

Calabrese, John. "China and the Persian Gulf: Energy and Security." *Middle East Journal* vol. 52, no. 3 (Summer 1998).

Carnegie Endowment Study Group on Russia-China Relations. *Limited Partnership: Russia-China Relations in a Changing Asia* (Washington, DC: Carnegie Endowment for International Peace, 1998).

Chang, Maria Hsia. "Chinese Irredentist Nationalism: The Magician's Last Trick." *Comparative Strategy* vol. 17 (1998).

Chari, P. R. *Indo-Pak Nuclear Standoff: The Role of the United States* (New Delhi: Manohar, 1995).

Cheng, Joseph. "China's Foreign Policy in the Mid-1990s." *Strategic Studies* (India) vol. 19, no. 1 (Winter 1996/97).

Chopra, V. D. *Pakistan and Asian Peace* (New Delhi: Patriot Publishers, 1985).

Choudhry, G. W. *India, Pakistan, Bangladesh, and the Major Powers* (Free Press, London: Collier Macmillan Publishers, 1975).

Christensen, Thomas. "Chinese Realpolitik." *Foreign Affairs* vol. 75, no. 5 (September/October 1996).

Christensen, Thomas J. and Jack Snyder. "Chain Gangs and Passed Bucks: Predicting Alliance Patterns in Multipolarity." *International Organization* vol. 44, no. 2 (Spring 1990).

Cohen, Stephen P. *The Pakistan Army* (Karachi: Oxford University Press, 1998).

Cortwright, David and Amitabh Mattoo. *India and the Bomb: Public Opinion and Nuclear Options* (Notre Dame, IN: University of Notre Dame Press, 1996).

Deng, Yong. "Managing China's Hegemonic Ascension: Engagement from Southeast Asia." *Journal of Strategic Studies* vol. 21, no. 1 (March 1998).

Dong, Yeng. "The Chinese Conception of National Interests in International Relations." *The China Quarterly*, no. 154 (June 1998).

Downing, John. "China's Maritime Strategy." *Jane's Intelligence Review*, Parts 1 & 2 (March and April 1996).

Durrani, Asad. *Pakistan's Security and the Nuclear Option* (Islamabad: Institute for Policy Studies, 1995).

Economist Intelligence Unit. *EIU Country Report: China, Mongolia* 2nd Quarter 1998, Country Profile 1998-1999.

Ehteshami, Anoushiravan. *The Changing Balance of Power in Asia*. Emirates Occasional Paper no. 16 (Abu Dhabi: Emirates Center for Strategic Studies and Research, 1998).

Faust, John R. and Judith F. Kornberg. *China in World Politics* (Boulder, CO: Lynne Rienner Publishers, 1995).

Freedman, Lawrence (ed.) *Strategic Coercion: Concepts and Cases* (Oxford: Oxford University Press, 1998).

Garrett, Banning N. and Bonnie S. Glaser. "Chinese Perspectives on Nuclear Arms Control." *International Security* vol. 20, no. 3 (Winter 1995/96).

Garver, John. "Sino-Indian Rapprochement and the Sino-Pakistan Entente," *Political Science Quarterly* vol. 111, no. 2 (1996): 323–347.

Ghosh, Suchita. "Impact on India of the China-Bangladesh Connection." *Strategic Analysis* (August 1994).

Gilpin, Robert. *War and Change in World Politics* (New York, NY: Cambridge University Press, 1981).

Godwin, Paul H.B. "Uncertainty, Insecurity, and China's Military Power." *Current History* (September 1997).

Goldstein, Avery. "Great Expectations: Interpreting China's Arrival." *International Security* vol. 22, no. 3 (Winter 1997/98).

—"China in 1997: A Year in Transition." *Asian Survey* vol. 38, no. 1 (January 1998).

Government of India. Department of Science and Technology, *Research and Development Statistics 1994–95* (New Delhi: The Offsetters, 1996).

Graham, Norman A. "China and the Future of Security Cooperation and Conflict in Asia." *Journal of Asian and African Studies* vol. 23, no. 1 (1998).

Guoxing, Ji. "China versus South China Sea Security." *Security Dialogue* vol. 29, no. 1 (1998).

Hoodbhoy, Pervez. *Islam and Science: Islamic Orthodoxy and the Battle for Rationality* (London: Zed Books Ltd, 1991).

Hussain, Irtiza. *Strategic Dimensions of Pakistan's Foreign Policy* (Lahore, Progressive Publishers, 1989).

Hussain, Mushahid. *Pakistan and the Changing Regional Scenario: Reflections of a Journalist* (Lahore, Progressive Publishers, 1988).

International Security, Proliferation and Federal Services Subcommittee. *China: The Proliferation Primer* (Washington, DC: United States Senate Committee on Government Affairs, January 1998).

Kayahara, Ikuo. "China as a Military Power in the Twenty-first Century." *Japan Review of International Affairs* (Spring 1998).

Kennedy, D. E. *The Security of Southern Asia* (London: Chatto & Windus, 1965).

Keohane, Robert O. and Joseph S. Nye Jr. *Power and Interdependence*, 2nd Edition (Boston, MA: Scott Foresman, 1989).

Kim, Samuel S. "China as a Great Power." *Current History* vol. (September 1997).

Klintworth, Gary (ed.) *Asia-Pacific Security: Less Uncertainty, New Opportunities?* (New York, NY: St. Martin's Press, 1995).

Kodikara, Shelton U. *South Asian Strategic Issues: Sri Lankan Perspectives* (New Delhi: Sage Publications, 1990).

Krepon, Michael (ed.) *Defense and Insecurity in Southern Asia* (Washington, DC: Henry L. Stimson Center, 1995).

Lai To, Lee. "East Asian Assessments of China's Security Policy." *International Affairs* vol. 73, no. 2 (1997).

Liu, Xuecheng. *The Sino-Indian Border Dispute and Sino-Indian Relations* (Lanham, MD: University Press of America, 1994).

Magnus Ralph H. and Eden Nabi. *Afghanistan: Mullah, Marx and Mujahid* (Boulder, CO: Westview Pres, 1998).

Malik, J. Mohan. "India Goes Nuclear: Rationale, Benefits, Costs and Implications." *Contemporary Southeast Asia* vol. 20, no. 2 (August 1998).

—"China's Policy Towards Nuclear Arms Control: Post-Cold War Era." *Contemporary Security Policy* vol. 16, no. 2 (August 1995).

—"China-India Relations in the Post-Soviet Era: The Continuing Rivalry." *China Quarterly* no. 142 (June 1995).

Mandelbaum, Michael (ed.) *The Strategic Quadrangle: Russia, China, Japan, and the United States in East Asia* (New York, NY: Council on Foreign Relations Press, 1995).

Mansfield, Edward D. and Jack Snyder. "Democratization and the Danger of War." *International Security* vol. 20, no.1 (Summer 1995).

Mearsheimer, John J. "Back to the Future: Instability in Europe after the Cold War." *International Security* vol. 15, no. 1 (Summer 1990).

Melet, Yasmin, "China's political and economic relations with Kazakhstan and Kyrgyzstan." *Central Asian Survey* vol. 17, no. 2 (1998).

National Defense University. *Strategic Assessment 1998: Engaging Power for Peace* (Washington, DC: National Defense University Press, 1998).

Nathan, Andrew J. and Robert S. Ross. *The Great Wall and the Empty Fortress: China's Search for Security* (New York, NY: W.W. Norton, 1997).

Nye, Joseph S. "China's Re-emergence and the Future of the Asia-Pacific." *Survival* vol. 39, no. 4 (Winter 1997-1998).

Overholt, William. *The Rise of China* (New York, NY: Norton, 1993).

Palit, D. K. and P. K. S. Namboodiri. *Pakistan's Islamic Bomb* (New Delhi: Vikas, 1979).

Pollack, Jonathan and Richard H. Yang (eds) *In China's Shadow: Regional Perspectives on Chinese Foreign and Military Development* (Santa Monica, CA: RAND, 1998).

Porteous, Holly. "China's View of Strategic Weapons." *Jane's Intelligence Review* (March 1996).

Reiss, Mitchell. *Why Countries Constrain their Nuclear Capabilities* (Baltimore, MA: The Johns Hopkins University Press, 1995).

Rizvi, Hasan Askari. *The Military and Politics in Pakistan* (Lahore, Progressive Publishers, 1974).

Robinson, Thomas W. and David Shambaugh (eds) *Chinese Foreign Policy: Theory and Practice* (Oxford: Clarendon Press, 1994).

Rosenau, James N. (ed.) *International Politics and Foreign Policy*, 2nd Edition (New York: NY, Free Press, 1969).

Ross, Robert S. "Beijing as a Conservative Power." *Foreign Affairs* vol. 76, no. 2 (March/April 1997).

Roy, Dennis. "Current Sino-US Relations in Strategic Perspective." *Contemporary Southeast Asia* vol. 20, no. 3 (December 1998).

— "China's Threat Environment." *Security Dialogue* vol. 27, no. 4 (1996).

Schultz, John J. "China as a Strategic Threat: Myths and Realities." *Strategic Review* (Winter 1998).

Shahi, Agha. *Pakistan's Security and Foreign Policy* (Lahore, Pakistan: Progressive Publishers, 1988).

Singh, Jasjit (ed.) *Light Weapons and International Security* (Pugwash: IDSA, 1995).

—(ed.) *Nuclear India* (New Delhi: Knowledge World, 1998).

Singh, Ravinder Pal (ed.) *Arms Procurement Decision Making, Volume I: China, India, Israel, Japan, South Korea and Thailand* (Oxford: Oxford University Press, 1998).

Singh, Swaran. "China's Changing Maritime Strategy: Implications for Indian Ocean Region." *Journal for Indian Ocean Studies* vol. 5, no. 1 (November 1997).

—"Sino-Indian CBMs: Problems and Prospects." *Strategic Analysis* (India) (July 1997).

Shiying, Pan. *Reflections on Modern Strategy: Post-Cold War Strategic Theory* (Beijing: Shijie Zhishi Chubanshe, 1993).

Sperling, James, Yogendra Malik and David Louscher (eds) *Zones of Amity, Zones of Enmity: The Prospects for Economic and Military Security in Asia.* (Leiden, E.J. Brill Publishers, 1998).

Sreedhar. "China Becoming a Superpower and India's Options." *Strategic Analysis* (India) (July 1997).

Syed, Fasahat (ed.) *Nuclear Disarmament and Conventional Arms Control Including Light Weapons* (Rawalpindi: FRIENDS, 1997).

Tahir-Kheli, Shirin. *India, Pakistan and the United States: Breaking with the Past* (New York, NY: Council on Foreign Relations, 1997).

United States Department of Defense. *East Asian Strategy Report 1998* (Washington, DC: Government Printing Office, 1998).

Walker, William. "International Nuclear Relations after the Indian and Pakistani Test Explosions." *International Affairs* vol. 74, no. 3 (1998).

Walt, Stephen M. *The Origins of Alliances* (Ithaca, NY: Cornell University Press, 1988).

Waltz, Kenneth. *Theory of International Politics* (Menlo Park, CA: Addison-Wesley, 1979).

Wang, Hongyu. "Sino-Indian Relations, Present and Future." *Asian Survey* vol. 35 (1995).

Weinbaum, Marvin G. and Chetan Kumar (eds) *South Asia Approaches the Millennium: Reexamining National Security (*Boulder, CO: Westview Press, 1995).

Zhang, Yongjin and Rouben Azizian (eds) *Ethnic Challenges beyond Borders: Chinese and Russian Perspectives on the Central Asian Conundrum* (London: Macmillan Press Ltd., 1998).

Ziring Lawrence. *Pakistan: The Enigma of Political Development* (London: Dawson Westview, 1980).

Newspapers & Journals

Dawn, Karachi, 1997-1998

Die Zeit, Hamburg, 1998

Far Eastern Economic Review, Hong Kong, 1997-1998

India Today, 1996-1998

Margalla Papers, National Defence College, Islamabad, 1997-1998

Nation, Islamabad, 1997-1999

National Development and Security, Foundation for Research on International Environment National Development and Security (FRIENDS), Rawalpindi, 1998

News, Islamabad, 1998-1999

Pakistan Horizon, The Pakistan Institute of International Affairs, Karachi, 1997-1998

Regional Studies, Institute of Regional Studies, Islamabad, 1998

The Guardian, London, 1997-1998

Time (Weekly), New York, 1997-1998

Index